PREVENTING EATING DISORDERS AMONG PRE-TEEN GIRLS

PREVENTING EATING DISORDERS AMONG PRE-TEEN GIRLS

A Step-by-Step Guide

Beverly Neu Menassa

Westport, Connecticut
London

Library of Congress Cataloging-in-Publication Data

Menassa, Beverly Neu, 1965–
    Preventing eating disorders among pre-teen girls : a step-by step guide / by Beverly Nue
Menassa.
        p. cm.
    Includes bibliographical references and index.
    ISBN 0-86569-332-3 (alk. paper)
        1. Eating disorders in children—Prevention. 2. Eating disorders in adolescence—
Prevention. 3. Girls—Health and hygiene. 4. Children—Health and hygiene. I. Title.
RJ506.E18M46 2004
618.92'8526—dc22   2004043772

British Library Cataloguing in Publication Data is available.

Library of Congress Catalog Card Number: 2004043772
ISBN: 0-86569-332-3

First published in 2004

Praeger Publishers, 88 Post Road West, Westport, CT 06881
An imprint of Greenwood Publishing Group, Inc.
www.praeger.com

Printed in the United States of America

The paper used in this book complies with the
Permanent Paper Standard issued by the National
Information Standards Organization (Z39.48-1984).

10 9 8 7 6 5 4 3 2 1

To my husband Bret and my son Garrett
—my love, my inspiration, my laughter

CONTENTS

———————————————•———————————————

Acknowledgments   xi

Preface   xiii

Chapter 1   **Literature Review**   1
             Brief Historical Overview and Diagnostic Criteria   1
             Etiology   3
             Prevention Theory and Prevention Programs   11
             Body Armor   14

Chapter 2   **Rationale for Risk Factors**   17
             Media Literacy   17
             Body Image and Self-Esteem   19
             Dieting and Nutrition   20
             Stress and Coping Resources   22

Chapter 3   **Overview of the Body Armor Program**   25
             How to Use This Guide   25
             Target Audience   26
             Psychoeducational Groups and the Leader's Role   29
             Structure of the Group   29
             Session Overviews   30
             Using the Appendixes   32
             Using Computer-Assisted Interventions   32
             Parental Involvement   32
             Selection of Group Members   33

	Training the Cofacilitators	34
	Evaluation Method	35
	Ethical and Multicultural Issues Anticipated	36

Chapter 4   **Sessions**   39
            Session 1: Taking a Closer Look   39
            Session 2: Having a Voice   42
            Session 3: Scales Are for Fish   44
            Session 4: Coping with Stress, Part I   47
            Session 5: Coping with Stress, Part II   48
            Session 6: Body Image   50
            Session 7: Putting It All Together   53
            Session 8: *The More You Know*   55
            Session 9: Becoming the Teacher   57
            Session 10: Parental Involvement   58

Appendix A   **Forms and Questionnaires**   61
            Permission Form   62
            Goals and Objectives of the Body Armor
                Prevention Program   62
            Confidentiality   63
            Questionnaire for Parent or Guardian   64
            Children's Version of the Eating Attitudes Test   65
            Cofacilitator Evaluation of the Group Leader   67
            You Are Invited!   69

Appendix B   **Taking a Closer Look**   71
            About-Face: http://www.about-face.org   73
            Breaking-the-Code Activity   75

Appendix C   **Having a Voice**   77

Appendix D   **Scales Are for Fish**   79
            USDA Food Guide Pyramid   80

Appendix E   **Coping with Stress**   81
            Websites for Session 4: Coping with Stress, Part I   82
            Websites for Session 5: Coping with Stress, Part II   82
            My Pledge   83
            Breathing and Meditation Exercises   84

Appendix F   **Body Image**   87
              Meet Cindy Jackson   88

Appendix G   **Putting It All Together**   89
              Anorexia Nervosa   90
              Bulimia Nervosa   90
              Session 7: Activity Information   91

Appendix H   *The More You Know*   93
              The More You Know Scripts   94

Appendix I   **Resource Materials for Parents and Guardians**   95
              Handouts   96
              Empowering Websites   96
              Eating Disorders Resources   98

References   101

Index   109

ACKNOWLEDGMENTS

———————————— • ————————————

I would like to express thanks to the following individuals: Dr. Richard Maeder, who initially challenged me to begin such an endeavor; Dr. Ann Lynch, professor and friend, who provided constant support and encouragement throughout the writing of this book; Robin Truhe, friend and colleague who listened to all my concerns regarding this book; Dr. Changming Duan, the first to encourage me on the road to counseling clients; and all the young women with eating disorders whom I have counseled over the years—you were inspirational to this book and to my life.

PREFACE

———————————— • ————————————

I remember when I first began hearing about eating disorders: it was through the media, soon after Karen Carpenter died in 1983 of heart failure caused by chronic anorexia nervosa. After her death, anorexia and bulimia became the topics of after-school specials and made-for-television movies. I remember watching the first movie ever made about anorexia nervosa, *The Best Little Girl in the World,* starring Jennifer Jason Leigh. This movie had a powerful effect on me, and I knew I did not want to have anorexia, but I also knew I could relate to Casey Powell, the anorexic protagonist, and her desire to be thin. By age 15 I had already been on numerous diets, worn skintight girdles under my clothing, and become extremely dissatisfied with several parts of my body.

In the late 1980s and early 1990s, young girls with anorexia were regularly being paraded in front of live audiences on talk shows. Granted, these movies and daytime appearances brought attention to eating disorders and stimulated discussion, research, and treatment. However, I find it interesting that television producers no longer find this topic worthy of daytime television or movies. Why has this life-threatening disorder become commonplace? Why the fading interest by the media? The answer appears cynical but clear— young women with anorexia do not look much different from our favorite actors and models, so the shock value has lost its shock.

Nothing depicts this sentiment better than a story told by Adrienne Ressler, Clinical Outreach Director and Body Image Specialist at the Renfrew Center. I attended several seminars on eating disorders at which Ressler spoke at length about eating disorders and the media's influence on young women. She amazed the seminar participants throughout the day with statistics and information, but nothing was more telling or more interesting than a couple of anecdotes she told that had us all shaking our heads in disbelief. Ressler stated that a reporter from a national publication and her photographer arranged to interview several girls with anorexia who were receiving intensive, inpatient therapy at the Renfrew Center. Ressler allowed the interview, hoping to disseminate information in a major publication about the dangers of eating disorders. She carefully made all the arrangements, ensuring that a member of her staff was with the girls at all times. Toward the end of the interview, the reporter and photographer found a way to get the girls alone. The photographer then whispered to the girls, "I don't care what anybody in here thinks. You both look fabulous." When the article and pictures of the girls were published, the magazine editor chose to place an advertisement depicting a waif-size model (thinner than the two girls who were struggling with a life-threatening illness) on the adjacent page.

Ressler told another story about a young girl who was nearing the end of her treatment at the Renfrew Center and was allowed an excursion outside of the center. The young girl went straight to the local mall. As she window-shopped, she noticed a sign in a sporting goods store: "Free Body Fat Analysis." Not many young women struggling with an eating disorder could resist such an offer. She went in, the clerk proceeded to check her body fat, and after he was done with his analysis, he told the young women to wait while he went and spoke with his manager. The manager of the shop rushed to shake hands with the young girl and, with somewhat of a flourish, presented her with an award for having the lowest body fat of all the customers they had analyzed that month. The girl was rewarded for having an eating disorder!

When I began my studies to become a mental health counselor, I never dreamed I would want to specialize in eating-disorder treatment and prevention. The more I learned and the more accounts like those previously related that I heard, the more interested and angry I became. Treatment is difficult, painstaking, and intense, and the result can lead to health or, if unsuccessful, death. I worked with college women struggling with bulimia or anorexia. There is no denying the intensity of the struggle. Once the disorder has taken hold, recovery is long and arduous—an average of seven years, followed by a lifetime of coping. As I researched treatment options and became overwhelmed with literature—books, journal articles, pamphlets, and websites—on the topic, my interest turned to prevention. As I read studies and investigated different programs that focused on the prevention of eating disorders, I knew I wanted to contribute to this endeavor. I wanted to create a prevention program in the hope that fewer young college women would enter my office wanting desperately to be released from the grip of their eating disorder.

My journey began, intending to find, or at least to theorize, the disease's source and then to develop a prevention program based on this theory. This book is the culmination of that journey.

Beverly Neu Menassa
February 22, 2004

1

LITERATURE REVIEW

—•—

Being a woman is hard work. . . . The woman who survives intact
and happy must be at once tender and tough. She must have
convinced herself, or be in the unending process of convincing
herself, that she, her values, and her choices are important.

—MAYA ANGELOU

This first chapter will briefly discuss how various theoretical perspectives view
the etiology of eating disorders. You may find that you agree or disagree with
a number of perspectives. At times, you may agree with parts of one theory
but emphatically disagree with other ideological statements. This is expected.
Please understand that this prevention program was developed based on my
theoretical perspective of the etiology of eating disorders, a perspective that
will be thoroughly explored throughout this book.

Also, before you implement the Body Armor prevention program, it is important to understand eating disorders from a past and a present perspective.
By assuming the role of group leader or cofacilitator, you are immediately put
in the position of expert; therefore, having a good knowledge base will better
prepare you to lead or cofacilitate this program, answer a multitude of questions, and cope with situations as they arise.

BRIEF HISTORICAL OVERVIEW AND DIAGNOSTIC CRITERIA

It is an interesting fact that well before anorexia nervosa became a documented disorder, humans were starving themselves, and some received much

notoriety if the restriction of food was done for self-denial or as a sacrifice for the achievement of spiritual redemption. Self-starvation for religious atonement occurred from the Middle Ages until it was finally recognized as a disorder in the late 1800s. Sir William Gull in England first documented the physical symptoms of anorexia nervosa and, at about the same time, Charles Laseque in France made note of the emotional disturbances of the person with anorexia (Kinoy, Holman, & Lemberg, 1999).

Since Sir William Gull's and Charles Laseque's discoveries, literally thousands of articles, personal accounts, books, and Web pages have been generated, all focusing on eating disorders. Many mental health professionals have attempted to determine a cause, and their best efforts have only produced numerous speculations. It is fortunate that much is known about the physical and emotional characteristics and about risk factors; unfortunately, very little is known about protective factors and about the relationship between risks and disturbances. What is known are the characteristics of the disorder, and those that involve body image disturbance are quite intriguing; the other symptoms may simply be a result of this disturbance and the weight loss. The diagnostic criteria of anorexia nervosa are as follows:

- The individual refuses to maintain a healthy body weight and fears gaining weight although she is already underweight, defined as less than 85 percent body weight of what is expected at any given time and during periods of growth;
- The individual has an unrealistic view of her body image—a misinterpretation of her actual body size and a denial of the severity and dangerousness of the weight loss;
- The individual, if developmentally at an age at which she is menstruating, misses at least three successive menstrual cycles. (American Psychiatric Association, 2000, p. 589)

Common characteristics of anorexia nervosa include:

- fasting, vomiting or laxative use;
- hyperactivity;
- rituals and obsessive compulsive thoughts surrounding food and exercise;
- depression;
- growth of fine body hair;
- decreased blood pressure;
- slowed heart rate;

- electrolyte imbalance;
- dental problems;
- and/or death. (Kinoy, Holman, & Lemberg, 1999)

The individual with anorexia nervosa believes she can perfect herself by perfecting her body and, thus, receive public admiration and acceptance. She has a distorted body image and is incapable of listening to her body's needs and viewing her body from a realistic perspective. If left untreated, the individual may die because she simply cannot control it.

Although individuals with a diagnosed eating disorder share similar cognitions, bulimia nervosa may present quite differently from anorexia nervosa; however, an individual may show symptoms of both. The symptoms of bulimia nervosa were first documented in 1959 and, in 1994, the American Psychiatric Association classified bulimia nervosa as a separate disorder. This disorder's diagnostic criteria are as follows:

- The individual has episodes of binge eating, which is characterized by eating amounts of food in a prescribed period of time that would be larger than what others would consume in the same timeframe;
- The individual has a lack of control of eating—she feels as if she cannot stop eating;
- The individual uses compensatory behaviors such as self-induced vomiting, laxative use, or excessive exercise to prevent weight gain; this binge and compensatory-behavior cycle occurs at least twice a week during a three-month period; and
- The individual judges herself based on her weight and body shape. (American Psychiatric Association, 2000, p. 594)

ETIOLOGY

Psychodynamic Theory

Different theoretical models view eating disorders as stemming from different psychological, environmental, biological, and sociological factors. For example, Hilda Bruch (1978), in her groundbreaking work with girls with eating disorders, views the disorder from a psychodynamic approach and postulates that there is usually some defining event that serves as a trigger for eating disturbances. A girl may see herself in a photo, she may be exposed to inconsiderate comments from a doctor or parent, or she may suffer teasing about her weight from peers. However, Bruch states that this defining moment is preceded by inner conflict or an impasse about self-acceptance. An impasse can occur at any time during the young girl's development. For example, a young girl may be sent away to camp and feel unsure about making friends, or she may have an overwhelming feeling of being out of control of her body as puberty kicks in, or she may experience changes and feel ill-equipped to cope with them. A change might be a sibling going away to college, the family moving to a new neighborhood, a divorce in the family, a family member becoming ill, and/or sexual trauma (Bruch, 1978). Bruch also posits that many girls wish to stop their developing bodies and remain a child, protected and engulfed by their parents' love forever.

The psychodynamic model also suggests that young girls perceive the masculine body as the more desirable form; therefore, they begin to see their own bodies as unacceptable, undesirable, deficient, or flawed (Dare & Crowther, 1995). Furthermore, during the phallic stage, young women notice they lack a penis and attempt to perfect their bodies by preventing the unacceptable feminine form from developing (Dare & Crowther, 1995). In essence, by starving themselves, young girls have rejected their femininity hoping to achieve the more ideal form—a masculine body type. Freud's theory also suggests that during the oedipal stage, young women may fear an actual or imagined incestuous relationship with their fathers, so to avoid this, they develop an anorexic (androgynous) shape.

Overall, psychodynamic theory explores how young girls with eating disorders interact with their environments. The symptoms these girls develop indicate maladaptive ways of coping with their changing environment. Psychodynamic therapists explore these symptoms to gain access to the underlying disturbances that helped create the eating disorder (Johnson, 1995).

Genetic Model

In contrast to the psychodynamic theory, the genetic model posits that eating disorders run in families. Studies conducted on twins provide support for this theory; findings show that the genetic predisposition for the disorder is more significant among the families of girls with anorexia nervosa than with those families with bulimia nervosa (Treasure & Holland, 1995). Another researcher (Strober, 1995) examined six genetic studies that showed girls with anorexia nervosa or with bulimia nervosa were several times more likely to have a relative with the disorder. Strober also found that girls with eating disorders were more likely to have a family member with a history of depression, bipolar disorder, and/or substance abuse. However, he does caution the reader not to get too optimistic about the genetic research; the path to an eating disorder is not a straight one and multiple variants play a role.

Family Model

The family model believes that the family plays a role in the development of an eating disorder, but not necessarily on a genetic level. The family model posits that families that are excessively close or over-involved, not allowing the adolescent to individuate and separate, may encourage anorexic behavior (Eisler, 1995). This theory also speculates that girls who are anorexic may come from overly controlled and overly organized families, while the girls who are bulimic may have been raised in families that are more conflicted, critical, or chaotic (Vandereycken, 1995). In addition, young women may be more susceptible to eating disturbances if their mothers are overly concerned about their daughters' appearance and weight or if their fathers are withdrawn, ineffectual or uninterested in their daughters (Eisler, 1995). A lack of supporting evidence makes it difficult to support the aforementioned claims; however, there is evidence to support the claim that negative events in the family (i.e., sexual abuse, divorce, death of a parent) puts young women at risk for developing an eating disorder.

One particular negative event, sexual abuse, has been the topic of numerous studies attempting to determine a causal link between childhood sexual abuse (CSA) and eating disorders. In a 1997 study, researchers S. A. Wonderlich, T. D. Brewerton, Z. Jocic, B. S. Dansky, and D. W. Abbott reviewed twelve studies to determine if CSA was a precursor to eating disorders. Out of the twelve studies, eight studies (Bushnell, Wells, & Oakley-Brown, 1992; Calam & Slade, 1989; Dansky, Brewerton, Kilpatrick, & O'Neil, 1997; Garfinkel & Lin, 1995; Hastings & Kern, 1994; Miller, McCluskey-Fawcett, & Irving, 1993; Steiger & Zanko, 1990; Wonderlich & Donaldson, 1996) supported the hypothesis that CSA is related to the development of an eating disorder. To understand the link between the two, the authors posit that CSA creates internal conflict and, quite possibly, post traumatic stress disorder. Girls may develop bulimia nervosa or anorexia nervosa as a way to avoid coping with the sexual abuse. In essence, thinking about the abuse becomes too difficult, so girls with eating disorders can limit their thinking to their present and immediate world of food.

Women who have been sexually abused describe their purging behavior as a way to void the perpetrator from them, to rid themselves of the rage they feel toward their attacker, and to relieve themselves of the shame, guilt and dirty feeling they have toward their own bodies (Costin, 1999). Those who binge but do not purge gain extra pounds to protect themselves against any future attacks. In addition, women with eating disorders may view being overweight or underweight as a protective measure, creating a body that is quite asexual and unattractive to a potential predator or partner (Costin, 1999).

Developmental Theory

One of the most important developmental factors that affects young girls is puberty. This is a confusing time for both girls and boys; however, girls tend to feel more out of control of their bodies as their bodies develop the necessary fat (hips and thighs widen, breasts grow larger) for them to become mature, sexual women. Girls receive numerous messages from magazines, television, billboards, and so on that any amount of fat is unacceptable. Therefore, feeling out of control, girls will often look inward and attempt to control their bodies. Dieting begins, disordered eating patterns emerge, and girls become at risk for developing an eating disorder.

Striegel-Moore (1995) views this developmental stage as a time when girls acquire their "relational self." Young girls learn that their worth is inexorably tied to their ability to form meaningful relationships with others. In essence, their self-worth depends on the formation of these relationships, and they are judged by others regarding their success or failure of these unions. Failing to form these relationships leaves girls feeling inferior, worthless, and anxious. Girls realize that being physically attractive will assist them in maintaining relationships and this is when the disturbed eating habits emerge. Girls may then try to fit in by dieting to strive for the socially acceptable shape— extreme thinness. The cycle begins with dieting behavior that can lead to disordered eating, which can progress to an eating disorder (Striegel-Moore, 1995). Targeting the prepubescent girl for an eating disorder prevention program may help prevent this cycle from ever beginning (Friedman, 1998).

Pipher (1994) makes some interesting and quite poignant observations about developing girls. She states that girls lack the ability to think abstractly and tend to overgeneralize information they hear. For example, a young girl may know of one friend who gets to stay up until midnight and her dramatic response to her parents might be, "But everyone gets to stay up until midnight." One example turns into "everyone," and the young girl truly believes it is "everyone" except her. In the same vein, girls tend to view themselves as absolutely fabulous one day and an absolute geek the next day. Pipher remarks that girls may be on top of the world one day and in the gripes of despair the next. One bad grade or one ugly, insensitive comment can set off a major emotional crisis for a girl. Again, like thinking, feelings are black or white with no room for the gray. "Girls have tried to kill themselves because they were grounded for a weekend or didn't get asked to the prom" (Pipher, p. 57). One casual remark from a parent, teacher, or a physician will be interpreted with significant meaning—prophetic meaning. For example, one negative comment about a girl's breasts, legs, thighs, hips, stomach, and so forth can be agonizing for the young girl. She may spend more time obsessing over the perceived imperfection than studying or talking to friends, or interacting with her family. In some instances, that one comment, or series of comments, gets buried in the girl's subconscious and, ultimately, she may embark on a lifelong struggle to lose inches off those hips or thighs or whatever body part in her mind's eye is not quite right. Puberty, in the Western culture, is not celebrated, is not honored, is not admired. There are few, if any, coming-of-age rituals to recognize the burgeoning woman within. It seems there are more jeers than cheers for girls as they enter this wondrous time of their lives. As teachers, parents, and counselors, it is important to be sensitive and hyper-aware of the cognitive and emotional concrete world that girls are attempting to traverse each day.

Biochemical Theory

The biochemical theory supporters view eating disorders from a different perspective. Scientists have discovered that the neurotransmitters seratonin and norephinephrine function abnormally in individuals with depression and with anorexia and bulimia. Binge eating may be a young girl's way of coping with the depression. Scientists have also found that those with eating disorders have a biochemical in the brain similar to individuals with obsessive-compulsive disorder (OCD). Individuals with OCD and individuals with an eating disorder both have been found to have an abnormal amount of the hormone vasopressin in their brains. This hormone is released in response to physically and emotionally stressful situations. Furthermore, the hormone cholecystokinin (CCK) is low in some women with bulimia. This hormone produces a satiation response; therefore, women with bulimia who have deficient levels of CCK may continue to binge, not able to discern that they feel satisfactorily full. Finally, the neuropeptide Y and peptide YY stimulate eating responses in rats, and research shows that theses peptides are elevated in women with anorexia and bulimia (Robinson & McHugh, 1995).

Cognitive Behavioral Model

On the other hand, the behavioral component of the cognitive behavioral model posits that eating disordered behaviors are learned. For example, a young girl goes on a diet and loses ten pounds. She is rewarded by parents, friends, even teachers telling her how wonderful she looks. She is rewarded by a society that values thinness. She rewards herself on her self-control. All this positive reinforcement leads to positive feelings and increased disordered eating behaviors that result in more weight lose and more positive reinforcement. By continuing to diet and lose weight, she avoids negative reinforcement (De Silva, 1995). The cognitive component of this model goes further and explores how the girl thinks about her weight, her body shape, and her food choices and consumption. Behaviorally, she is already conditioned to see the "importance" of being thin, so she develops the faulty cognitions to support her behaviors. She may think, "I am worthy and special if I am thin." "I will be unhappy if I gain any weight." "If I eat one cookie it will immediately be converted to fat." In some girls, the disordered eating behaviors develop into a full-blown eating disorder. Now, friends and family are telling the girl she is too thin and needs to gain weight. Unfortunately, it is too late. The girl has become increasingly isolated and her internal voice becomes more important than the external voices extending negative reinforcement. Her anorexia has taken on a life of its own (De Silva, 1995). The pattern of behavior and the dysfunctional thinking are well established and eradicating them will be difficult.

Another cognitive behavioral theorist suggests that the causes of eating disorders should be viewed in two ways—the risk factors that are present to help create the disorder and, once established, the behaviors or cognitions that maintain the disorder (Fairburn, 1995). The road to an eating disorder may have various routes and there is no one single cause. For example, possible causes may include, dieting, social factors, gender, age, genetic links, trauma, and comorbidity issues (Fairburn, 1995). However, once disordered eating patterns begin to take shape, it is the all-or-nothing thinking, the cognitive distortions regarding body image, and the already existent negative self-image that help to create the actual eating disorder (Fairburn, 1997). The girls, judging themselves harshly, hope to feel better when they lose weight. Unfortunately, the cognitive distortions will continue, contributing to a cycle of negative self-assessment, which leads to more attempts at weight loss.

The Feminist Model

All of the aforementioned models agree that sociocultural factors play a mediating role in the development of eating disorders; however, the feminist model insists that cultural factors play a primary role in the etiology. Research shows that eating disorders are rarely found in non-Western societies, are more common among women than men, and have increased during the past thirty years. Also, many women display the symptoms of eating disorders (obsessive dieting and restricting of foods, body image concerns, etc.), but they may never be diagnosed with the syndrome. Unfortunately, today's women are engaging in disordered eating patterns, are overly concerned about body image, and are making unrealistic demands on a media-induced image of their "perfect," "malleable" bodies. As a result of all these symptoms of eating disorders and of the increased numbers of young women developing eating disorders, many feminists and others in the helping professions are seeking the answer to several philosophical questions (Dolan & Gitzinger, 1994).

Why now (Dolan & Gitzinger, 1994; Streigel-Moore, 1995)? Feminists note that when women have progressed in their personal lives and in the political arena, society's standards for beauty also progressed to the extreme— "extreme thinness" (Dolan, 1994). In the 1950s, the incidence rate of anorexia nervosa was 7 per 100,000 persons; in the 1980s, this increased to 26.3 with the average age of onset for young women at 14.6 (Steiner & Lock, 1998). One theory is that a thin body represents women's reproductive freedom and is a symbol of progress toward liberation. Women no longer need a father, brother, or husband to take care of them—to feed them. However, others view this "cult of thinness" as a reaction to women's increased power. If women are constantly worried about their weight, they will worry less about achievement. Thus, they will be controlled, take up less space in society and, finally, conform to traditional values. Failure to achieve the desired weight loss contributes to lower self-esteem in women. Women question their worth, and ultimately, feel powerless (Dolan, 1994).

Why women (Dolan & Gitzinger, 1994; Streigel-Moore, 1995)? Women place a greater significance on interpersonal relationships and are taught from a young age that beauty is important in finding and keeping a mate (Dolan, 1994). Marriage and/or having a mate is so esteemed, so valued in our society that this value is reflected in the so-called reality television genre that is currently taking over prime-time network television. It is interesting that young women are willing to go on television and be *Married by America*, spar for a *Millionaire*, be courted by men in masks, and ogled by the average "Joe." Is this another backlash to women's independence (Faludi, 1991)? Is this another attempt to push women back into the traditional role of the 1950s? Does the term "old maid" ring a bell? Beauty is sold to girls in the toys they play with, the magazines they read, and the shows they watch. Women now vie to go on television and allow a panel of judges to decide if they are "hot or not." The prettier girl is often depicted as the smarter, the more competent, the more idealized. The problem with this is that girls are being forced into a role they may not wish to inhabit and are being sold a narrow definition of beauty they will not be able to attain.

Considering that women and girls view 400 to 600 advertisements each day, with one out of every eleven ads directly communicating a beauty message, we can begin to understand how our definition of beauty has become so narrow (Dittrich, 1996). Television advertisements contribute directly to this narrow definition and indirectly to eating disorders by promoting women as objects for men's pleasure. For example, when both men and women are portrayed in an advertisement, men are more likely to look directly and unabashedly at a woman, possibly judging body features; women are usually portrayed viewing men in a covert manner. For example, the "Diet Coke Break" ad that came out in 1994 shows women taking an 11:30 A.M. Diet Coke break to ogle a handsome construction worker who strips off his shirt and has a Diet Coke. The construction worker, interestingly, strips off a pink T-shirt before drinking the Diet Coke. Why pink? He is taking on the traditional female role of being ogled by men. Although somewhat groundbreaking for women to enjoy and to judge a man's body, the women must do this in a covert manner. The construction worker doesn't know he is being watched.

In a similar Hanes commercial, two women are surreptitiously guessing which men are wearing briefs and which men are wearing boxers. When Michael Jordon confronts the women, they giggle with embarrassment at having been caught looking at the men's bodies. Commercial after commercial depicts women in the role of being judged and watched, whether she is showing off her shiny new hair or eating Doritos. In contrast, the men ogle overtly (women know they are being watched), and the men in the ads rarely, if ever, act embarrassed at having been caught in the act of ogling. The message is clear—women are always on display; women are always being watched; women's perfect appearance is expected. Life is one big Miss America Pageant (Pipher, 1994). The message that women are valued for how they look is being driven home each and every day.

In addition to television shows and commercials doing damage to young girls' psyches, fashion magazines deliver a similar blow. These magazines depict the perfect woman that all women should aspire to be. Interesting studies have been conducted to measure the self-esteem of a woman after she views a fashion magazine that depicts the thin ideal of beauty. These studies have found women feel less attractive and less confident, and they express feelings of shame, guilt, depression, body displeasure, and anxiety after viewing images from these magazines (Irving, 1990; Richins, 1991; Stice & Shaw, 1994). As young girls mature, they are more likely to compare their bodies to those of fashion magazine models (Martin & Kennedy, 1993). Sadly, models' body weight run approximately 15 percent below their recommended weight, and many girls, striving for this thin ideal, will be unable to achieve the unachievable and will face a life of self-loathing, starvation diets, anxiety, and disordered eating.

PREVENTION THEORY AND PREVENTION PROGRAMS

Disorder-Specific Continuity Model

Although the etiology of eating disorders is still speculative, practitioners and researchers have moved forward with prevention efforts. Several prevention models have been postulated, including the Disorder-Specific Continuity model, which is a psychosocial or social learning approach. It views disordered eating along a continuum and suggests that there are many similarities from one end of the continuum (some concerns about weight) to the other end (a diagnosable eating disorder). These prevention programs want to assist parents, teachers, coaches, and other significant adults in the girls' lives to help eliminate the precipitating factors (dieting, negative body image, low self-esteem, excessive exercising, etc.) and to increase the girls' overall ability to resist the allure of these precipitating factors (Levine, 1999).

Nonspecific Life Stress Model

A second model, the Nonspecific Life Stress model, focuses on reducing stressors to decrease risks for emotional disorders. Decision-making skills, communication skills, and techniques to cope with stress are taught to increase self-esteem.

Feminist Model

The feminist model not only provides young women with information about the media, body image, dieting, and so on, but it also is designed to empower "girls and women to change (create) themselves and their environments" (Levine, 1999, p. 67).

Programs that provide young women with a place "to decode the language of fat," to develop a positive sense of themselves, and to encourage support systems are relatively successful (Friedman, 1998, p. 220). However, research has indicated that the media contributes to our thin ideal of beauty and leads to increased dieting behaviors (Berel & Irving, 1998). Learning to feel good about one self is useful but is insufficient armor for the preadolescent girl. She needs to become media literate to decode the messages imbedded in the 400 to 600 ads girls are exposed to each day (Dittrich, 1996). Prevention programs work best if they empower girls (and women) to change their environments. Young women need to learn that they not only have a voice in a small, safe, subsystem provided by a group leader, but that they also have a voice in a larger system—society. Granted, girls need to have a place to talk and share their feelings about the negative messages they receive, but they also need to learn to be active in changing the world around them. Given these tools, the girls may acquire the necessary body armor to interact in the Western culture.

Nutrition Model

Many prevention programs have focused solely on nutrition. Studies have since indicated that programs designed to eliminate unhealthy eating patterns usually are unsuccessful. Students increase their knowledge base, but rarely do they change their eating attitudes or weight regulation habits (Berel & Irving, 1998). There is also the concern that these types of programs may inadvertently reinforce the very behaviors they want to eliminate by providing knowledge on how to engage in unhealthy eating practices. Similarly, it seems rather paradoxical to teach girls to eat healthy when society is telling them not to eat or to feel guilty and diet if they do eat; or to teach "girls to accept their body image" and not address "how society encourages them to dissociate from their bodies"; or to encourage self-esteem in a society "that does not esteem girls" (Friedman, 1998, p. 218). Prevention programs that focus on a variety of risk factors, including the media's influence on shaping attitudes about the thin ideal, may be more effective than a program focused simply on healthy and unhealthy eating patterns (Berel & Irving, 1998).

Risk Factors

In the past ten years, there has been considerable focus given to determining risk factors for eating disorders. Ghaderi (2001) conducted a review of the literature and discussed the current philosophy related to risk factors, provided information concerning the implications of prevention programs, and made suggestions for future programs. Ghaderi reviewed twelve possible risk factors, including sociocultural factors, dieting, body dissatisfaction, self-esteem, social support, coping, teasing, being overweight, perfectionism, family interaction and environment, stress and life events, and depression. He concluded that more research is necessary; however, he found that the current literature supports the creation of prevention programs based on the aforementioned risk factors. This will be discussed in more depth in chapter 2.

Universal and Target Programs

Interestingly, Dalle Grave (2003) conducted an evaluation of 29 prevention programs used in the past 10 years. He classified prevention programs in two categories: universal programs and target programs. Universal programs target a group (i.e., specific school and grade level) of willing participants, despite the classification of low-risk or high-risk individuals. On the other hand, target programs focus on a specific group identified as high-risk for developing a certain behavior or disorder. Dalle Grave further classified prevention programs into early programs and second-generation prevention programs.

Early Models

One early model, the Nonspecific Vulnerability Stressor model (NSVS), assumes that there are many indirect paths to developing an eating disorder—no direct path leads to the disorder. This model focuses on strengthening self-esteem, coping mechanisms, and overall acceptance of differences in people (Dalle Grave, 2003).

An additional early model, the Disease-Specific Pathways (DSP), views eating disorders as developing along a direct path and focuses on preventing and removing the risk factors to protect individuals from the disorder. The programs based on this model focus on a didactic approach and were successful at increasing knowledge but were not quite so successful at discouraging dieting behaviors or harmful attitudes related to body image (Dalle Grave, 2003).

Second-Generation Models

One of the second-generation models focuses on a dissonance-based approach, which encourages participants to be more interactive and to challenge prevailing beliefs about dieting and starvation imagery. A cognitive-restructuring model has also been employed to help change cognitions about the ideal body type. In addition, one model espouses the use of an Internet interactive psychoeducational program (Zabinsky et al., 2001), while one other model promotes the importance of increasing self-esteem as the most effective way to improve body image perceptions (O'Dea, 2001; O'Dea, 2002).

In his review of the 29 eating disorder prevention programs, Dalle Grave (2003) found that target programs had more positive results than universal programs. However, he did concede that it is more difficult to ascertain necessary data from a universal-type program that focuses on younger populations. Nine-to eleven-year-olds may not, as of yet, have engaged in dieting behaviors, so it is hard to measure a decrease in this behavior. He encouraged the development of more universal programs that are interactive in nature, connect knowledge to thoughts and actions, and link information from the classroom to the larger social environment by having the participants become activists.

Dalle Grave's (2003) review also found there is no statistical evidence to support the claim that some eating disorder prevention programs had caused harm to its participants as had been previously suggested in a study by Carter, Stewart, Dunn, and Fairburn (1997).

New Paradigms

There are several new paradigms for eating disorder prevention models (Dalle Grave, 2003). The Participatory-Empowerment-Ecological Relational (PEER) model includes many of the same basic ideological views of the DSP and NSVS models but views the program participants as the authority on their bodies and opinions. Adult mentors guide the discussion among the children and/or adolescents, but the knowledge base is derived from the participants. The information derived from the discussions can then be transformed into application. A second paradigm is the feminist approach discussed earlier that views education from an interactive and relational approach. The leader or facilitator of the group should be an adult female who can model behavior and impart information to the girls (Dalle Grave, 2003).

BODY ARMOR

The prevention programs used in schools thus far have had moderate success. Programs that focused on a didactic message or an interactive approach improved at least one attitude and at least one behavior in their participants (Dalle Grave, 2003). Of course, this varied among the programs. The Body Armor program will differ from the aforementioned programs in that it will integrate the PEER model and the feminist model. I have also incorporated aspects from the Disorder-Specific Continuity model and the Nonspecific Life Stress model. Not only will girls discuss the images they see in magazines and on television and explore their attitudes and feelings about specific images, but they will also become activists against starvation imagery in the media. Body Armor will challenge societal values and help girls find their voice to talk back to the television shows, the toys, and the ads. What do I mean by talk back? Let me give you an example that I distinctly remember from my childhood. As a nine-year-old girl I enjoyed watching beauty pageants. One evening I was glued to the television watching beautiful women parade around in bathing suits. My mother walked by, noticed what I was watching, briefly stopped in front of the television and, while looking at the television, commented, "Look at those women, being judged like a bunch of cattle." She then walked out of the room. I grew up on a farm and had been to the "sale barn"; I had observed firsthand the auctions where cattle were sold. I always felt sorry for the cows as they were brought out one by one to be judged and sold. The image my mother created for me was a powerful one. I never could look at pageants in the same way again. She didn't tell me to stop watching it. At that age I would have protested. The best thing she did was talk at the television, not at me!

The girls in the Body Armor program will be empowered to create themselves and change their environments, and will become the authorities as opposed to sitting and listening to a didactic message delivered by powerful experts. The girls will educate their parents, write letters to companies that present offensive ads, and create fact sheets about ways to cope with stress. By following this approach to prevention, this program will operate largely from the feminist model. However, I integrated the other models by focusing on the development of social learning skills (creating positive body images, increasing self-esteem, etc.) and by giving close attention to stress-reduction mechanisms. Body Armor will also address dieting and nutritional issues; however, it will spend much less time focusing on these topics—only one session—and will spend more time on promoting an acceptance of all body shapes.

One other unique feature of Body Armor is its focus on Internet activities. The girls will discover empowering websites designed just for them that they will access while participating in the program and may continue to access after the program concludes. This may help to strengthen the effects of the program and contribute to long-term attitudinal and behavioral changes.

Also, I have chosen not to focus directly on the topic of eating disorders. Although Dalle Grave (2003) discovered during his review that programs have not presented any threat or created harm to its participants, I decided to err on the side of caution. Discussing the compensatory behaviors of bulimia (i.e., laxative use, self-induced vomiting, etc.) may inadvertently teach the girls how to lose weight in unhealthy ways. Instead, I focus on concrete cognitions—how to cope with stress, how to choose healthy food, how to cope with teasing, how to resist media messages, how to become a watchdog against media messages that portray women negatively.

In addition, there are many activities built into this program that can be adapted by parents at home. Parents can accompany girls to the empowering websites (Appendixes E, G, and I), engage in frank discussions about the thin ideal relayed to us through the media, become team watchdogs (Appendixes B and C), do stress-relieving activities with their daughters, and together discuss nutrition and healthy food choices (Session 3). This collaborative effort could strengthen the overall results of Body Armor and, as mentioned earlier, could contribute to long-term attitudinal and behavioral changes, which, of course, is the ultimate goal.

2

RATIONALE FOR RISK FACTORS

---•---

The culture we have does not make people feel good
about themselves. We're teaching the wrong things. And
you have to be strong enough to say if the culture
doesn't work, don't buy it. Create your own.

—MORRIE SCHWARTZ IN *TUESDAYS WITH MORRIE*

MEDIA LITERACY

Research supports that the media has influence on young girls and women,
and increased exposure to media's message of the drive for thinness may be
directly related to the development of eating disorders (Berel & Irving,
1998). For example, after young women viewed fashion magazines, they had
an increased desire to imitate the thin-is-beautiful standard (Levine, Smolak,
& Hayden, 1994). Furthermore, after viewing slides of extremely thin models, many women reported lower self-esteem, decreased satisfaction with their
own bodies, increased depression, shame, guilt, and stress (Dittrich, 1996).
Another study found that women experienced more pressure from the media
to adhere to standards of thinness than from their own friends or family,
which implies that the message to be thin is being delivered more frequently
and with more verve in the media (Berel & Irving, 1998).

It is interesting that when we are continuously exposed to a message, it becomes a part of our being and to think a different way becomes difficult
(sounds a lot like brainwashing). There is a similar phenomenon that occurs
with other species. For example, say you had an aquarium with several fish.
When you first brought the fish home, you placed a barrier in the middle of

the fish tank, restricting the fish movement to only one side of the tank. The fish explored and learned the size of their home. If you remove the barrier, the fish will not venture to the other side of the tank. It has become impossible for them to view their existence in any other way (Ressler, 1999). If the fish could talk, they might ask, "How can that side of the tank be available to me now? Why would I want to venture to that side of the tank?" Women experience similar barriers in our society, and if we were to remove the barrier of the thin ideal of beauty, women might ask, "How can my body, a size 16, be beautiful? Every message I received from little on told me it could not be beautiful unless it were a size 2. How can dieting be dangerous? I've been told through thousands of media messages that I must diet." Can women change how they think about beauty and dieting? Of course they can, but it takes some effort to combat a deeply embedded message. Fortunately, we are much smarter than fish. The hope is, though, that by teaching young girls to become media literate, they will not have this same struggle and will be more satisfied with their bodies and, ultimately, will avoid disordered eating behaviors.

These deeply embedded messages are also being delivered under the guise of a toy for young girls. I had a Barbie when I was five years old and, if I recall correctly, all my friends had Barbies. I remember dressing her and studying her body, and I know I was not consciously thinking this is the ideal woman's figure, but I am sure this insidious message was creeping its way into my mind. In fact, one study found that 90 percent of young girls in the United States own or have owned a Barbie, whose figure, we know, is proportionately unattainable (Dittrich, 1996). Barbie has changed considerably over the years. Her hips have widened, her breasts are smaller, and her clothing reflects the current fashion scene. Mattel continually competes with the new trends and works to keep Barbie hip. The new My Scene Barbie sports halter tops, short shorts, short skirts, flared jeans, and so on, and all bare Barbie's belly. Of course, she is incredibly, unbearably thin, with long flowing hair, wearing an unseemly amount of makeup, promoting the thin ideal, sex-sells message (Creager, 2002). A few years ago my niece received a Diva Starz Nikki Doll (another Mattel invention) for Christmas. Nikki's main purpose in being is to help young girls learn about fashion. When she talks her oversized lips light up and she blinks her huge eyelashes, revealing startling eyeshadow. She makes comments about fashion, and provides girls with a word of the day, such as sweeterrific. I found the doll a little frightening. Something about the oversized head, eyes, and lips felt disconcerting to me; however, my niece seemed to love it. Again, the message is the same. Girls should focus on their looks, not their intellects, even at seven years of age.

Media literacy interventions may reduce the negative, influential effects of the toys girls play with and the messages they receive via the media by promoting critical thinking (Berel & Irving, 1998). Moreover, several studies found that after a media intervention program was conducted, children's attitudes about the importance of the media successfully changed (Austin & Johnson, 1997; Austin & Meili, 1994). However, programs need to go one step further; they need to attack media messages at their core and enact and promote change, which is central to prevention efforts (Wright, 1996). Without this change, prevention programs will simply exist to detect behaviors already well established (Wright, 1996).

Body Armor will spend a considerable amount of time exploring media messages and teaching the girls to become media literate. The program does go one step further—it deals with societal change. The girls will become activist/watchdogs and will find ads that present women in a negative light. They will write letters to companies expressing their concerns. The hope is that when these girls become women, they won't need to ask the question, "How can my body be beautiful?" They will know they are beautiful, whatever their size. And, perhaps, with girls becoming activist and shouting NO to starvation imagery, the media will change how it portrays women.

BODY IMAGE AND SELF-ESTEEM

Body image and self-esteem are interrelated; a misperception in one, more than likely, will result in a distortion in the other. "If one dislikes one's body, it's difficult to like the person who lives there" (Cash & Strachan, 1999, p. 33). Being thin in our society means more than just being attractive; it now connotes success, and those who are thin, successful, attractive, and feminine can be viewed as having succeeded in achieving "the American Dream." No longer is the Mercedes or the big home the sole determiner of status. Thin is in, and it is a status symbol! The premise being packaged and delivered to us daily is that thin women are upper class and upwardly mobile and women with curves and more voluptuous physiques are lower class and downwardly mobile (Fedoroff & McFarlane, 1998). To achieve this ultimate status, many women resort to some very painful measures: liposuction, lower facelifts, upper facelifts, mask facelifts, nose jobs, silicon breast implants, removal of silicon breast implants, chemical peels, chin reductions, cheek implants, laser forehead resurfacing, eye widenings, hair transplants, collagen lip injections, permanent makeup, and so on. Feminist-model promotes combating negative body image by challenging gender roles and shifting girls' attentions from an external view of their bodies to a more internal view of their gifts and abilities (Srebnik & Saltzberg, 1994).

The feminist model also believes that current standards for beauty, as well as a sociohistorical perspective, should be examined. As women advanced economically and politically, they were circumscribed psychologically by physical perfection. For example, securing the vote in 1920 was juxtaposed with the flapper look. The boyish haircuts, thin physiques, and rebellious attitudes of the flappers represent women's increased freedom; however, this freedom came at a cost. Women had to forego their womanly bodies, de-emphasize curves, breasts, and all semblance of reproductive physiques. The feminist movement of the 1960s was accompanied by the top model, Twiggy, appearing weak, asexual, and hungry, and by today's standard, her five-foot-eight, 97-pound frame would be considered anorexic. Having models emerge weak and powerless appears to be a direct backlash to women's attempts to gain equality (Faludi, 1991). The 1980s saw "the hunger cult" (Naomi Campbell, Cindy Crawford, and Elle McPherson) as women's roles in society continued to increase. It is interesting to note that, after World War II, women returned to their domestic roles, and Marilyn Monroe became the top female model and actor of the time. As a five-foot-five, 135-pound, size 14 woman, Monroe clearly symbolized that it was acceptable to be full figured. Although valued solely for her body, Monroe's buxom shape may have had a direct affect on the decreased number of cases of anorexia. Statistics reveal that during the 1950s, the number of women with anorexia significantly decreased from 16 per 100,000 persons in the 1930s and 1940s to 7 per 100,000. The number increased to 26.3 per 100,000 in the 1980s (Steiner & Lock, 1998).

In addition to the feminist model, art therapy is an effective means for girls to explore their preoccupation with their bodies. One particular technique, often used with individuals with eating disorders at the Renfrew Center of Florida, may also be quite effective in a prevention program. Large roles of paper are strewn about, and girls are asked to draw a life-size outline of their body shape. After the girls draw their perceived body image, they are then asked to lie inside the outline. A partner will then trace their actual body outline within the borders of their perceived body image. Since almost all girls/women have, to some degree, a misperception of their bodies (Ressler, 1999), most will see that their actual size is smaller than their perceived size. This will provide a visual representation of negative body image, and by using the powerful medium of art, the girls' cognitions and feelings can be discussed.

DIETING AND NUTRITION

Gender roles in society devalue many qualities of women, yet emphasize appearance and a woman's ability to attract a mate above all others. Many young girls, when struggling with becoming a woman, receive the social message that to possess intelligence, to be powerful or masterful, or to be assertive will be viewed negatively by society, so to have some power, they may attempt to control their bodies. This is one way they can feel powerful. The messages they receive indicate that the ideal thin body can be achieved, their bodies are malleable, and if they really try, they too can change the genetic shape of their bodies and look like a supermodel. "Only in such a social situation where overconsumption is possible, or even too easy, can slimming become seen as a luxury and a desirable activity" (Dolan, 1994, p. 4).

The diet industry feeds off women's insecurity, and "despite the fact that its success is built upon its customers' failures" (Dolan, 1994, p. 2), Americans spend approximately $35 billion dollars a year on dieting products (Ressler, 1999). One study found that when women were told they could have three magic wishes, not surprisingly, 75 percent wished for weight reduction (Kilbourne, 1995). Quite astoundingly, 80 percent of 10-year-olds have dieted or are currently dieting (Kilbourne, 1995). Sixty-five million individuals are currently struggling to lose weight through some form or diet (Bloom, Gitter, Gutwill, Kogel, & Zaphiropoulos, 1999), and 50 percent of women, disliking the bodies they see in the mirror, join the struggle on a daily basis (*Body Image*, 2000). Another astounding statistic centers around the low success rate of diets: 95 percent of people who lose weight on a diet gain back the weight within three to five years (Bloom et al., 1999; Dolan, 1994). Nevertheless, dieting is the norm and now seems to be a rite of passage into womanhood. Rarely do people question, and almost everyone accepts, the young woman's desire to diet. The woman who doesn't diet or worry about her weight is viewed as the abnormal one. It is unfortunate that dieting may lead to bingeing, bingeing may lead to a feeling of a loss of control, and the dieting behavior may begin again to regain that control.

This cycle is dangerous; dieting may be a risk factor and a precursor to the development of bulimia nervosa (Mussel et al., 1997). Although we now know that dieting can lead to disordered eating behaviors, young women still engage in these behaviors at alarming rates. A little more than 15 percent of the high school and college women surveyed could be diagnosed with an eating disorder, and 4.3 percent could be classified as anorexic (Cavanaugh & Lemberg, 1999).

Poor nutrition may lead to a multitude of other problems for kids, such as iron deficiencies, undernutrition, dental caries, and decreased resistance to infectious diseases. It may also affect the cognitive development of young children, resulting in poor concentration, learning, and overall academic achievement (Perry, Story, & Lytle, 1997). And, that is not all. Poor nutritional patterns that develop in childhood may be carried into adult years.

Coronary heart disease, some cancers, diabetes, and strokes are leading causes of death in adults and these diseases relate directly to individuals' diets (Perry, Story, & Lytle, 1997). Obviously, spending so much time restricting certain foods (the premise behind dieting), and then, perhaps, bingeing on the forbidden foods, could contribute to the development of certain diseases.

Body Armor will help the young girls understand the danger and the futility of dieting behaviors. They will be introduced to the natural solution—no foods are off-limits. Denying oneself of a certain food immediately creates a magical quality surrounding that food, and a binge episode could be triggered (Bloom et al., 1999). This program will encourage these young women to begin to listen to their bodies (Bloom et al., 1999), to eat when they are physiologically hungry, and to recognize the feeling of satiation. This program will also teach girls to begin thinking differently about the foods they consume. This will not be an easy task. Our society, without a doubt, has food issues. We now have senators and congresspersons deciding if foods high in fat should be taxed—a fat tax—similar to the so-called sin tax placed on cigarettes and alcohol. Once again, a message is being delivered—certain foods are "bad," and somehow all our food issues can be solved if we just make the foods more expensive. Are foods really good or bad? Are we good if we eat a salad and bad if we eat a Hostess cupcake? This prevention program will attempt to change cognitive processes surrounding food and suggest an alternate way of viewing foods. It will also help girls develop the necessary life skills to decode the many dysfunctional messages about food delivered to them daily.

Finally, this prevention program will also ask its participants to view the media to understand how it encourages women to use food in emotional ways, to indulge in certain foods, and then to diet to avoid gaining weight. One study (Silverstein, Perdue, Peterson, & Kelly, 1986) found that in 48 different issues of women's magazines there were 63 advertisements about diet foods; in 48 issues of magazines directed toward men they found one ad. Comparably, another study (Anderson & DiDomenico, 1992) discovered that women's magazines contain about 10 times more dieting ads and weight-loss articles than did men's magazines. The Body Armor program will help young women interpret the messages they are receiving about food and dieting.

STRESS AND COPING RESOURCES

Preadolescents experience stress from numerous sources in their lives. For example, life-event stressors such as divorce, remarriage of parents, death of a parent, interpersonal relationships, conflict with teachers, the transition into puberty, and so on are viewed as problems that arise for children and adolescents. These life-event stressors can be categorized into daily stress, home and family stress, school stress, and developmental stress (Miars, 1996). Because many of these stress factors are unavoidable for youths, coping strategies are needed to buffer their effects.

Several models have been proposed to connect life-event stressors to eating disorders. The cumulative stressor model suggests that adolescents who experience an inordinately large number of stressful issues are at risk for developing eating disorders. On the other hand, the traumatic life events model proposes that those who develop eating disorders are people who have been exposed to abuse, neglect, death and so on. The normative stressor model indicates that it is not necessarily the stressor that could predict disordered eating behaviors, but rather it is the perceptions of the stressful events that make the difference whether individuals will be susceptible to eating disorders (Sharpe, Ryst, Hinshaw, & Steiner, 1997). There is some evidence to support the normative stressor model; however, the research is rather sparse at this time. Therefore, preadolescent girls must be taught coping skills to reduce their vulnerability to cumulative, traumatic, or normative stressors.

Body Armor will attempt to introduce girls to stress-reduction strategies. Folkman and Lazarus (1985) classified ways of coping into eight coping scales: problem-focused, wishful thinking, distancing, seeking social support, emphasizing the positive, self-blame, tension reduction, and self isolation. Tension reduction can be taught to the girls through the use of progressive muscle relaxation and visual imagery, two techniques that have been shown to be effective with children (Miars, 1996). The girls can be taught to modify the stressors (problem-focused approach) and to manage their emotional response to the stressor by emphasizing the positive and by seeking social support. One study found four coping strategies—problem-focused, seeks social support, avoidance, and wishful thinking—were used most among adolescents (Halstead, Johnson, & Cunningham, 1993). Girls in the study were more likely to seek social support and defer to wishful thinking than boys (Halstead, Johnson, & Cunningham, 1993). Having at least one healthy relationship with a significant adult can provide the necessary body armor a child needs to combat the effects of stress (Miars, 1996). The Body Armor program will help the preadolescent girls identify stressors, explore how they have attempted to cope with these stressors in the past, and generate effective ways to deal with stressors in the future.

3

OVERVIEW OF THE
BODY ARMOR PROGRAM

———————————— • ————————————

If our children are to approve of themselves,
they must see that we approve of ourselves.

—MAYA ANGELOU

HOW TO USE THIS GUIDE

When viewed statistically, eating disorders take on an epidemic-like quality. "Eating disorders rank as the third most common chronic illness among adolescent females in the United States" (Neumark-Sztainer, 1996, p. 2). The facts themselves demonstrate the need for an eating-disorder prevention program: recovery is long and expensive, only 40 percent of girls and women ever completely recover from an eating disorder, one-third of the women continue on with unhealthy eating behaviors, and 20 percent do not recover to any degree. Mortality rates can be as high as 10 percent, resulting from suicide, starvation, or cardiac arrest (Neumark-Sztainer, 1996). My primary reason for creating Body Armor is to help prevent eating disorders in preadolescent girls by helping them develop stress-coping resources, increase self-esteem, explore their own specific body-image issues, investigate the harmful effects of dieting, learn healthy ways to view food, gather nutritional information, and develop interpretive skills pertaining to media messages.

This chapter will provide an overview of the Body Armor program, including brief discussions about the target audience for the program, group theory and the structure of the group, session overviews, using the appendixes, using computer-assisted instruction, parental involvement in the program, and selection of group members. Read through this chapter carefully. Understanding group selection, the structure of the group, and the order of the sessions will become quite important once you begin the process.

TARGET AUDIENCE

Once I knew that I wanted to focus my attention on preventing eating disorders, I had to consider the age group to target. The onset of puberty has often been considered the catalyst for eating disorders. Frequently, anorexia and bulimia nervosa will emerge in young women between the ages of 14 and 18, and by the time young women reach high school, disturbed eating behaviors appear quite normal to them and are much more difficult to eradicate. "One reason that prevention programs aimed at adolescents are unsuccessful is that they are begun too late" (Friedman, 1998, p. 218). Should all girls, no matter where they are on the continuum, be included in a prevention program, or should only at-risk girls participate? One study found that all girls benefit from such a program, although prevention programs may not have the power to modify already existing behaviors (Neumark-Sztainer, 1996). Another study found that preadolescent girls may have well-defined ideas about acceptable body shape and these perceptions may already be influencing behavior; however, this may be the time when attitudes are most malleable (Sands, Tricker, Sherman, Armatas, & Maschette, 1997). This study (Sands et al., 1997) also found that body-image perception develops well before puberty; therefore, targeting preadolescent girls may have the most success for an eating-disorders prevention program.

Putting all the studies aside, I decided to conduct some experiential research. Where better to experience preadolescent attitudes than at my local mall? I spent an entire Saturday afternoon observing and listening in girls' clothing departments in several large department stores. The first thing that surprised me was the type of clothing being sold to girls ages 9 to 12. Jeans were flared or low rise or both; blouses were shear, sparkly, short at the midriff. I spend a lot of time in the boys' section of stores because I have a little boy, so I rarely, if ever, venture into the girls' department. It was interesting to note that the clothing, unlike boys' clothes, seemed sexually charged. I found myself feeling grateful I had a boy. How do parents cope and compete with the pressures from the media advertising these types of sexually charged clothes as "must haves" and "cool"?

Next, I listened to what girls had to say about the clothing. Again, I was surprised how grown-up they sounded. I heard comments like, "This will look so cute on me." "This outfit will make me look so cool." "Mom, do you think this makes my butt look too big?" "I wish I were a smaller size." After reading and analyzing numerous studies and after hearing these somewhat disturbing comments, my decision was an easy one—this prevention program would target girls ages 9 to 12 years old.

After deciding on an age group, I needed to decide on gender. Should boys be included in the program? Because statistics show that there is a 19-to-1 ratio of females to males who have been diagnosed with an eating disorder, I chose to exclude boys when creating this prevention program (Jones, 1997). You may choose to include boys, but be aware that the program was written with girls in mind, and boys in this age group may be somewhat of a distraction for the girls. On the other hand, they may be able to reinforce some of the points being made. Because males are not immune to eating disturbances, their inclusion could be beneficial to them and to the girls. One study found "that girls aspired to thinner body shapes than boys found to be attractive" (Neumark-Sztainer, 1996, p. 67). However, other studies revealed that boys were not interested in the subject matter and were more of a disturbance than a positive force (Neumark-Sztainer, 1996).

Thinking about the program in terms of ethnicity, I realized that the stereotypical view of the individual with an eating disorder is a middle- to upper-socioeconomic status, young, White woman (Wright, 1996). These disorders have, unfortunately, become viewed as a "culture-bound syndrome," meaning eating disorders and eating-disorder symptoms are confined to individuals in one specific culture (Jacob, 2001). However, other cultures are affected by eating disorders but are less diagnosed or are misdiagnosed because of this stereotypical misperception. For example, the prevailing view suggests that African Americans have certain values embedded within their culture that protect them from developing eating disorders. Such values include an acceptance of larger body types and a decreased drive for thinness (Petersons, Rojhani, Steinhaus, & Larkin, 2000). However, new studies have indicated that as more African American women enter the middle class and become pressured by the dominant culture's beliefs, they will experience the same societal demands to be thin and will be more susceptible to developing eating disorders (Abrams, Allen, & Gray, 1993; Demarest & Allen, 2000). Demarest and Allen found that African American women were as dissatisfied with their body size as were Caucasian women.

Hispanic women have also demonstrated increasing dissatisfaction with their bodies. Gowen and Hayward (1999) studied acculturation with Hispanic girls and how language spoken in their homes and number of years in the United States affected the development of eating disorders. Not surprisingly, they found that a higher level of acculturation might increase rates of eating disorders among Hispanic girls. Another study looked at Latino American women who recently immigrated to the United States and found that low self-esteem and a strong desire to be accepted by the prevailing culture may contribute to increased body dissatisfaction and eating disorders (Pate, Pumariega, Hester, & Garner, 1992). *Real Women Have Curves*, an HBO film, explores this idea of the level of acculturation and need for acceptance by the American culture.

In the film, Ana, an 18-year-old Mexican American woman living in East Los Angeles, must choose between her mother's idea of living the American dream—being thin, working hard, marrying young, and having children, and her own desire to go away to college and become independent. Throughout the film, Ana's mother refers to Ana as her "butterball," insists Ana lose weight, and tells her she should be ashamed of her size. In one poignant scene, Ana challenges her mother and says, "You're overweight." Her mother's response is, "Yes, but I'm married." Toward the end of the movie, when the heat in the sweatshop where Ana, her sister, and her mother work becomes unbearable, Ana takes off her clothing and stands free and unashamed in her bra and panties. Her mother is outraged and tries to cover her. During the course of a conversation about cellulite and stretch marks, a comparison ensues and within minutes all the women, except Ana's mother, are working and dancing in their bras and panties. One of the women exclaims, "Look at us. We are beautiful." The trailer for the movie reads, "Real women take chances, have flaws, embrace life . . . and have curves." I laughed out loud during this movie and found the slap-in-the-face attitude directed toward the mainstream drive for thinness refreshing. The studies listed previously are of the utmost importance in looking at Hispanic girls in relation to the prevalence of eating disorders; in addition, the movie helps give a face to these girls and women, demonstrating in a visual way that Hispanic women also struggle with body dissatisfaction.

Level of acculturation appears to play a role also with Asian American women. One study found highly acculturated Chinese students were more dissatisfied with their bodies (Davis & Katzman, 1999). Those who were less acculturated demonstrated less depression and fewer body issue concerns. Perhaps, like African American women, the Asian American culture provides some protective factors for women (Davis & Katzman, 1999). However, because studies show that being exposed to the Western value system may serve to increase vulnerability to eating disorders among all cultures, you will want to include girls of all ethnicities in this prevention program.

PSYCHOEDUCATIONAL GROUPS AND THE LEADER'S ROLE

If you are a teacher and you want to gather twenty girls and lead this psychoeducational group, you will want to involve an expert (school counselor) in the process (Gladding, 1999). You will still be in charge of leading all the group's activities, breaking the group into smaller subgroups, and managing the expert's role in the group (Gladding, 1999). The Association for Specialists in Group Work requires that leaders of psychoeducational groups have some advanced training; therefore, as a leader, you have several responsibilities that I have listed here:

1. Your role in a psychoeducational group will be to facilitate learning and skill development. You will serve as a teacher or instructor.
2. You should be familiar with research related to the content area (eating disorders). This manual was designed with this in mind and includes a sufficient amount of research material to assist you in becoming proficient in the area of eating disorders. However, teachers will be including an expert in the group process.
3. You also need to be skilled in selecting group members. Again, this manual addresses and instructs you on the best ways to select group members and cofacilitators.
4. You must be competent in designing structured sessions and exercises. This manual was designed for easy-to-use, step-by-step sessions and exercises for you to facilitate.
5. Most importantly, you should avoid invasion of privacy with "low-risk" members. Impart information but limit asking personal questions of the members.

STRUCTURE OF THE GROUP

Preadolescents are accustomed to classroom periods of 45 to 50 minutes in length. Therefore, this program consists of 10 sessions and each session is broken into two periods of 40 minutes each with a 10-minute break in between sessions. For the majority of sessions, the first 40 minutes can be held in a regular classroom equipped with a blackboard or dry-erase board and, possibly, a computer and projector. You may wish to conduct the last 40 minutes of most sessions in a computer-accessible room where the girls can work independently on the computers or in groups of two or three. Girls without computer knowledge can join girls who have the skills or can be assisted by you, a cofacilitator, or a lab technician. Depending on your school's curriculum and time allowed for psychoeducational groups, you may want to hold 20 sessions instead of 10. This can easily be done by stopping where the break is indicated and picking up the following day. However, if you choose to break up the sessions, remember to ease the girls into the next day's session with an introductory exercise and, perhaps, a recap of the previous day's focus and objectives.

SESSION OVERVIEWS

Each group session is focused on prevention by helping preadolescent girls develop stress-coping resources, body image and nutritional information, and interpretive skills pertaining to media messages. Chapter 2 presents the rationale for focusing on these specific prevention strategies.

I structured the sessions, keeping therapeutic factors and group stages in mind. The first five sessions will focus on activities that are more cognitively directed. Sessions 6, 7, and 8 will begin focusing on affect. By Session 6, as the group enters its working stage, the members should be more at ease in the group and more willing to disclose (Gladding, 1999). At this point, the sessions will become more productive now that members feel freer to try out new behaviors.

As you read through the manual, keep in mind that all sessions are arranged by explaining the session's *focus*, by exploring the session's *objectives* and the desired *behavioral outcomes*, and then by listing and detailing the particular session's *activities*, providing specific referrals to materials in the appendixes.

Session 1, titled *Taking a Closer Look*, is an informative group session, allowing the girls to become comfortable with you, the cofacilitators, and the other group members. Two activities and one presentation introduce the girls to embedded messages in advertisement and help them begin the process of decoding the messages. In this session, it is important for you and the cofacilitators to help the girls feel at ease and begin to gain their trust.

Advocacy is the focus of Session 2, titled *Having a Voice*. The goal of this group session is to help the girls understand that they have a voice. By participating in the group activity, the girls take a proactive stance against offensive and potentially unhealthy advertisements and write letters to the offending advertisers. You will need to follow up on the girls' letter-writing activity. Once a response to the letters is received, it should be shared with the girls to help generate feelings of empowerment.

Session 3, *Scales Are for Fish*, a title adapted from the Something Fishy website at http://www.something-fishy.org, focuses on the dangers of dieting and will attempt to change the way the girls view food as "good" or "bad." This view is reinforced by our society in a multitude of ads; however, food is not good or bad; it is sustenance. You and the cofacilitators need to be careful not to discuss your own dieting attempts and to refrain from biased comments about foods.

Sessions 4 and 5, *Coping with Stress* Parts I and II, teach the girls to identify stressful situations and to learn to cope with them. They will also learn about the body's physiological response to stress. During this session, you will teach the girls age-appropriate breathing and meditation techniques.

Session 6, *Body Image*, is one of the most important sessions. Many of the girls will get a visual representation of how they misperceive their actual size. You and the cofacilitators need to be extremely careful not to compartmentalize the girl's bodies or your own bodies. Comments such as "my thighs are much too large," or "my stomach pooches out too much," are harmful and prevent the girls from looking at their own bodies as a whole. You and the cofacilitators should discourage these types of comments among the girls and encourage them to view their entire body as a wondrous and beautiful entity, exploring all the things their bodies do for them each day.

Session 7, *Putting It All Together*, will help the girls understand that by coping with stress, avoiding dieting behaviors and eating healthy, decoding media messages, and by having a positive body image, they can feel healthy both physically and emotionally. You will need to play an active role in this session, helping the girls make the important connection between all they have learned and how important these strategies are to their overall health.

Session 8, aptly titled *The More You Know*, a title adapted from the Public Service Announcement series broadcast by the National Broadcasting Company (NBC), includes an empowering social change activity. This session builds on all the previous sessions and asks the girls to compose a public-service announcement for NBC's *The More You Know* ads. You and the cofacilitators will need to assist the girls in e-mailing their scripts to NBC.

Session 9, titled *Becoming the Teacher*, empowers the girls by letting them become the teacher. When we are asked to teach someone something, we become experts on the topic and seem to gain a better understanding of the material. The girls will be asked to prepare a skit or presentation for their parents or guardians. You and the cofacilitators should provide a significant amount of guidance during this activity. Another important part of this session is the topic of termination. The girls need to be allowed to have time to express their feelings about the group coming to an end and share the things they enjoyed or didn't enjoy about the group. You will need to guide the girls as they process their emotions.

Session 10 allows for *Parental Involvement*. The girls will be able to say goodbye and then present what they have learned to their parents. You will want to welcome the parents and present them with informational packets that focus on eating disorders and what behaviors, they, as parents, can change to help their daughters avoid developing an eating disorder.

USING THE APPENDIXES

The appendixes follow along with each session and provide illustrations of the topics being discussed or Internet addresses where you can go to locate appropriate illustrations. You may wish to create an overhead or make handouts so the girls have a clear visual of what you are discussing. You may also wish to locate additional examples to show the girls. Often the appendixes provide helpful tips about accessing computer information or provide resources for you or the parents or legal guardians. I have included in parentheses a quick reference to the appendix that is appropriate for the session.

USING COMPUTER-ASSISTED INTERVENTIONS

You and/or the cofacilitators will need to have some basic computer knowledge, so you can help the girls log on to the computer, assist them when they get on the Internet, guide them with the projects that require some word processing, and instruct them through the e-mail process. I have provided some easy-to-follow guidelines.

PARENTAL INVOLVEMENT

Studies indicate that prevention programs that include parents are more successful (Friedman, 1998; Rhyne-Winkler & Hubbard, 1994). Parental modeling is thought to play a role in the development of disordered eating behaviors; therefore, it is important that parents learn interventions that promote healthy eating, teach media skepticism, and model positive body image (Berel & Irving, 1998). Families can also model an acceptance of imperfection and be encouraged to keep communication open, especially to feelings, including anger. Families can also be taught to avoid placing too much value on their children's appearance; children may internalize negative messages about their bodies and place perfectionistic standards on themselves (Wright, 1996).

Body Armor encourages parental involvement. The girls' mothers and legal guardians are important to this program because young women need female role models who can share their own experiences with girls. However, the mothers who wish to participate will need to explore their own weight prejudices, and you may choose to exclude any mother currently on a diet from participating as a cofacilitator because the very behaviors being discouraged in the program could be reinforced by this individual. Furthermore, all the families will be asked to participate during the last session, which will be led by the participants. You may wish to give all families, regardless of participation, resource materials concerning how they might be contributing to another's eating disorder and how they can help prevent eating disorders.

SELECTION OF GROUP MEMBERS

Body Armor can be incorporated into the elementary and junior high school curriculum or can be used as a summer program by a junior high school, a community program, a community college or a university. Many colleges have summer programs for kids. Regardless of where the program is held, the sessions are structured to include 20 participants using four subgroups of five girls each throughout the sessions (Gladding, 1999). As the sessions progress, you may want to modify the subgroups, partnering different girls. This will all depend on the level of interaction that is occurring within the subgroups. If a girl appears to be left out and not participating, it will be worthwhile to change the subgroups.

Initially, you will want to either announce or advertise the group, or you may conduct the program with an already organized group of girls. How you choose to gather 20 girls ages 9–12 may depend on your school's policy.

After you have chosen your participants, invite the parents or legal guardians, who have expressed an interest in the program, and their daughters to a screening session at which the objectives of the group will be explained to them (Appendix A). Any that wish not to participate after the screening session may request that their daughters not participate in the program. This may happen, and it is always a good idea to have a list of interested participants on standby so that you can contact these girls and their parents. If you include a standby participant, you will need to explain program objectives to the parent(s) either in person or over the telephone. If the parent or legal guardian chooses to enroll his or her daughter after he or she has a good understanding of the group, it will be done at this time. If not, the next parent on the standby list will be contacted.

Ask the parents or legal guardians who attend the screening session to sign a permission form (Appendix A). Any parent who registers his or her daughter after the screening session will be mailed the permission slip and instructed that the form must be signed before her or his daughter can attend the first group session.

Explain confidentiality (Appendix A) to the girls. Although you will go over the importance of confidentiality during the first session, it is a good idea to begin the groundwork during the screening session. Carefully go over the information on the form in Appendix A. Many girls will not understand the meaning of confidential but will understand private. Avoid using the term "secret." This implies something covert is taking place in the group, and we don't want the girls to get the wrong impression or to be frightened. However, they do need to have an understanding of confidentiality and the limits of confidentiality.

Furthermore, screen the mothers and female guardians during the screening session to determine their level of interest in participating as cofacilitators in the group. All mothers and female guardians will be asked to complete a questionnaire (Appendix A). After the screening session, you can privately review their responses to the questions. Most of the questions on the questionnaire were taken from the Eating Attitudes Test that you will administer to the girls before the prevention program begins and after it is complete.

Administering this questionnaire to the mothers or female guardians will familiarize you with the test you will later administer to the girls. However, it will also provide you with some good insight into the mothers' and female guardians' prejudices about food and weight. The best candidates to serve as cofacilitators are those mothers who are interested in taking on the responsibility, who are not currently on a diet, and who are willing to explore their own weight prejudices. Of course, those who are willing to serve as cofacilitators and who answered "Rarely" or "Never" to the first eight questions would be ideal. Because we know that 50 percent of American women are dieting at any given time (*Body Image*, 2000), these first eight answers will more than likely range from "very often" to "sometimes." It will be your job to review the questionnaires and interview the interested candidates. This is a good opportunity to educate mothers and female guardians, which can also serve to prevent eating disorders. Approximately three to four mothers will be needed to assist with the group.

TRAINING THE COFACILITATORS

When you have administered the questionnaire and selected your cofacilitators, set up a time to meet with them as a group. At this meeting/

training session, share information about Body Armor's ideology concerning body image and eating disorders. Spend time going over the sessions with the cofacilitators so they have a good understanding of the structure of the group. Also, spend time cautioning the cofacilitators to avoid certain phrases or words about dieting. These women are role models for the girls and should refrain from talking about diets they have tried in the past (unless they are presenting personal accounts of how the diets did not work for them), about parts of their own bodies they don't like (compartmentalizing their bodies instead of seeing them as a whole), about foods that are "good" to eat or "bad" to eat, and so on. Spending an hour or two with the cofacilitators prior to the first group may eliminate the need to redirect them during the group meetings. However, as the group progresses, you may need to reiterate with the cofacilitators the theoretical perspective of the group and privately address any comments made by a cofacilitator that you deem inappropriate.

EVALUATION METHOD

To ascertain the overall effectiveness of the program, a pre- and post-test can be given to the group members. The Children's Version of the Eating Attitude Test (Appendix A) is a modified version of the Eating Attitudes Test and was designed to assess children's attitudes about body image, their obsessions with food, and their dieting practices. It is a 26-item questionnaire that is composed of a 6-point Likert scale. The standardization sample contained children who were between the ages of 8 and 13, were primarily White, and from middle- to upper-socioeconomic backgrounds (Babbitt, Edlen-Nezin, Manikam, Summers, & Murphy, 1995). The questionnaire's advantages are that it is easily readable and can be presented orally. However, the disadvantages of the instrument are that it has no reported validity data, and it may not be applicable to children from diverse ethnic backgrounds (Babbitt et al., 1995).

You may want to evaluate your effectiveness as the group leader; therefore, a second instrument, created by the author, can be used (Appendix A). The cofacilitators are asked to complete this questionnaire, which also contains a 6-point, Likert-type scale. The questions on this instrument pertain to group leadership skills, the organization of the group sessions, the leader's knowledge base, and the use of multimedia equipment. You can use the information ascertained by this instrument to improve the prevention program and your group skills.

ETHICAL AND MULTICULTURAL ISSUES ANTICIPATED

To ensure that ethical standards are upheld, you will want to provide the girls and their parents or guardians with information about the group's goals and objectives (Appendix A); the time parameters of the group; the fee for the group (if any); the members' roles, rights, and responsibilities; and any risks involved in joining the group.

There is limited risk in joining a psychoeducational group. One risk might be that a group member breaches confidentiality. Another risk might occur if a group member, trusting the group leader and/or group members, divulges information about depression, stress, abuse, and so on. If you are a teacher leading this group, defer to the expert you invited to be involved in the group. You or the expert will want to obtain the girl's permission to talk to her parents and then refer the girl to your expert, to another school counselor, or to a counselor in your community. Also, when feelings are being discussed, issues can arise. A risk might be a group member who explores her feelings, realizes she can trust you, tells you she is depressed and has been contemplating suicide. Once again, defer immediately to the expert participating in your group. The expert's (the school counselor) job is immediately to contact the girl's parents. There is no need to seek her permission to contact her parents, although doing so will help maintain your relationship with her. However, if she tells you she does not want you to contact her parents, explain to her once again the limits of confidentiality, tell her you are worried about her safety, and contact her parents. These types of concerns may not arise; however, understanding the risks involved and being prepared is important.

You will have "low-risk" girls and "high-risk" girls in your group. High risk means the girls have already developed some disordered eating behaviors; however, they do not have a diagnosable eating disorder. Low- and high-risk girls may equally benefit from the program.

You may have parents wanting their daughters who have eating disorders to join the group. This may not be the best group for the young girl. You may want to explain to parents that their daughter needs to be in individual and group counseling. If you choose to allow this girl in the group, be aware that the girl may disclose her disorder to the group during one of the activities. If you are a teacher leading this group, my advice to you is not to allow this girl to join the group. This type of disclosure to the group would be quite difficult to handle appropriately without proper training. However, you may want to discuss this with the expert you have invited to assist with the group to determine the appropriateness of having this girl in the group. If you are a counselor leading this group, weigh the advantages and disadvantages of having her in the group and then make your decision.

In addition to explaining risks, provide potential members and their parents or legal guardians with an opportunity to ask questions during the screening session to determine if the group is appropriate for their daughters. Furthermore, explaining confidentiality, the limits of confidentiality, and the attempts that will be made to uphold confidentiality of group members furthers the overall ethical nature of the group (Appendix A). Finally, the group leader and cofacilitators will take care to respect difference among the group members and to treat every member equally no matter the gender; cultural, racial, or religious affiliation; lifestyle choices; and/or disability (Gladding, 1999).

4

SESSIONS

---•---

Where did that woman in my mind come from?

—GLORIA STEINEM

SESSION 1: TAKING A CLOSER LOOK

The Focus

This first group session will concentrate on informing the girls about the structure, the purpose, the goals, and the rules of the group. This session will also focus on introductions. After this has been accomplished, the group will begin taking a closer look at the media and learning how to decode the messages embedded within. A feminist approach will be used and will focus on empowerment and gender issues.

The Objectives

The goals for this session are:

- to communicate structure, purpose, goals, and rules of the group;
- to help the girls begin to feel comfortable within the group by conducting an introductory exercise;

- to reduce the negative influential effects of the media by promoting critical thinking.

The Behavioral Outcomes

By the end of this session, the girls will have a better understanding about the group's purpose. They will understand how the group will be structured during the following weeks. They will also begin to develop different attitudes about the importance of the media.

The Activities

GREETINGS (7 minutes) Welcome the girls to the program; introduce yourself and the cofacilitators of the group. Inform the girls of the purpose of the group: to help them better understand the media, to help them become more accepting of a variety of body shapes, to help them eat better and live healthier lives, and to help them learn to cope with stress in their lives. Explain the structure of the group to them: two 40-minute sessions with one 10-minute break. Also, inform them that the second half of the class will often be held in a computer lab. Ask the girls who have not submitted their permission forms to do so at this time. Finally, discuss rules. Explain to the girls that they are to attempt to be on time for each group meeting. Then review the information on the form regarding confidentiality. Go over once again what types of information should be kept confidential (i.e., personal information about group members, personal information revealed in group sessions).

PRETEST (8 minutes) The girls will take the Children's Eating Attitudes Test. You may want to read each question aloud.

INTRODUCTORY EXERCISE (5 minutes) Explain the introductory exercise to the group members. A koosh ball (or some other type of ball) will be tossed around to each member. Only the girl holding the koosh ball will be recognized to speak. When holding the koosh ball, each girl is to say her name and one activity she enjoys that begins with the first letter of her name. For example, my name is Beverly and I like to read books. The koosh ball will be tossed to each member until everyone has a turn to introduce herself.

BRIEF PRESENTATION AND DISCUSSION (15 minutes) Introduce the girls to various models who have appeared in *Vogue* magazine (you may wish to purchase a *Vogue* magazine for demonstration purposes or go to the website at http://www.style.com and click on "People and Parties" to find examples of models) and ask the girls what they think about the models. Caution: Show only one or two photos of the models and do not show photos of celebrities. This may do more harm than good because the girls may already have postive feelings about certain celebrities. Also, showing too many photos of models may idealilze or glamorize the models, creating an adverse effect. A class discussion should follow, with you asking poignant questions:

- Where do you see fashion models?
- Have you seen models on television? In advertisements? In magazines?
- Why are models used in advertisements?
- What do you think about the models' sizes?
- How do you feel when you see a model?

ACTIVITY (5 minutes) Give the girls the sheet of numbers found in Appendix B. This activity is adapted from a workshop activity given by the Renfrew Center in Florida. They will be given one minute to connect the numbers (like a connect-the-dots game). Because of the amount of numbers and the chaotic structure of the numbers, they may not do very well in one minute. After the girls have worked for a minute, ask them if they would like to try again with the code for how to connect the numbers. On the second try, tell them that all the odd numbers are on the left-hand side of the page and all the even numbers are on the right-hand side of the page. They will have one minute to try again. After the minute is up, ask if they were more successful the second time because they knew the code. The group leader will introduce the concept of decoding media messages. Once the girls have the code, they can better understand the messages embedded within some of the 400 to 600 ads they see each day.

BREAK (10 minutes) The girls will be provided a healthy snack.

COMPUTER LAB (30 minutes)

The girls will then be introduced to the About-Face homepage (Appendix B). They will view the Gallery of Offenders (advertisements that present negative messages about women) on this homepage and they will see the Gallery of Winners (those advertisements that present women in a positive manner)

(Appendix B). One important aspect they will view on this homepage is the changes that have been made after consumers and organizations (like About-Face) have spoken up about how they feel about these advertisements. Caution: Some of the ads in the Gallery of Offenders are inappropriate for girls this age. Please refer to Appendix B for suggestions.

GROUP DISCUSSION, HOMEWORK ASSIGNMENT, AND CLOSURE (10 minutes) Ask the girls to become Watchdogs and bring to class advertisements that they feel present girls and women in both a negative and a positive way. The girls will be given an invitation (Appendix A) to give to their parents or guardians inviting them to the last half of the last session. The group will close with the koosh-ball activity, but this time the girls will say their names and then something they learned during Session 1 (e.g., "My name is Macie, and I learned advertisements can show women in a bad way.").

The Processing Questions

You will be able to ascertain the amount of information that the girls were able to process by attending to the closing activity.

SESSION 2: HAVING A VOICE

The Focus

This session will also focus on media literacy but will go the next step—advocacy. The theoretical approach is a feminist one, which incorporates aspects of the PEER model.

The Objectives

The goals for this session are:

- to help girls understand that they do have a voice and that that voice can make a difference;
- to encourage critical thinking skills;
- to express concerns about media messages that present women in a negative way;

- to celebrate media messages that send positive messages concerning women;
- to make changes in the social environment regarding how women are presented in the media.

The Behavioral Outcomes

The girls will learn that they can be advocates for girls and women in society. They will become better critical thinkers and will learn to decode media messages.

Activities

INTRODUCTION (3 minutes) Greet the girls and explain that the koosh ball will be tossed around and each girl should say her name and tell one positive thing that happened to her since the last session (e.g., "My name is Katelyn, and I scored a run in my baseball game.").

GROUP DISCUSSION (17 minutes) Have the girls form a circle and give them a chance to talk about the ads they located. Ask them to show the ads to the group and point out what they find offensive or potentially healthy about the ad.

SUBGROUPS (20 minutes) Now, create four groups of five. Instruct the girls to choose one negative and one positive ad from all the ads the subgroup members brought to share. After they have selected the ads, ask them to write two short letters about what they liked or didn't like about the ads. You and the cofacilitators may need to assist the girls in this endeavor.

BREAK (10 minutes) The girls will receive a healthy snack.

COMPUTER LAB (25 minutes) Help the girls post their letters at the About-Face website (Appendix C), at the National Eating Disorders website (Appendix C), or if the e-mail address can be found, directly to the company's advertising department. You and the cofacilitators will assist with this and check the e-mail daily to see if a response has been received.

CLOSURE (15 minutes) Using the koosh ball, the girls will be given a chance to discuss their feelings and thoughts about the day's activities (e.g., "My name is Robin, and I feel happy about writing a letter today."). Encourage the girls to continue to be Watchdogs and share their ads with the class during the next eight sessions.

The Processing Questions

- What does it mean to have a voice?
- Can one person make a difference?
- How does it feel to take a stand?

SESSION 3: SCALES ARE FOR FISH

The Focus

This session will focus on healthy eating. The slogan for it was adapted from the Something Fishy website at http://www.something-fishy.org. The model will be the Disorder-Specific Continuity model, which views dieting as a noxious agent that needs to be resisted.

The Objectives

The objectives in this session are:

- to provide information about healthy eating;
- to help girls learn to resist the urge to diet;
- to help girls learn that food is sustenance;
- to expose girls to the media's focus on women and food and women and dieting.

The Behavioral Outcomes

After this session, girls will understand the dangers of dieting, they will be able to decode the media messages that promote dieting, and they will learn to resist dieting and learn the natural solution to dieting.

The Activities

GREETINGS (10 minutes) While tossing the koosh ball from girl to girl, ask that each girl (when in possession of the koosh ball) say one thing that makes her feel proud about herself (e.g., "I can run fast; I like to do math; I make good cookies; etc."). If you feel everyone knows everyone's name, you can forgo having the girls state their names before their statement. After the koosh-ball activity, ask the girls to share any ads that they have found.

GROUP DISCUSSION (30 minutes) Show the girls a picture of Alicia Machado, Miss Universe 1996. (An image of Machado can be located at http://www.pageant.com/universe96/index.html.) She gained weight after winning the title and was told by Donald Trump she would need to go on a diet or lose her crown. Ask the girls the following questions:

- What do you think about this request?
- Is Ms. Machado no longer beautiful and able to represent Miss Universe if she gains 20 pounds?
- How do you think Ms. Machado felt about this request?
- What message does this send to girls and women?
- Has anyone ever told you you were too fat or too thin? How did this make you feel?
- How could you respond if someone teases you about your body or weight?

Show the girls the cover of a *Woman's World* magazine and address the contradictory message on the cover. One particular cover (located at www.ccgdata.com/8786-52.html or at www.4magazines.net/8786-52.html) promises women that they can not only reach their "dream weight," but can also "bake up some happiness!" The magazine basically tells women they need to diet while showing them pictures of chocolate cake and delectable cookies. This cover also ties emotion to food. Baked food leads to happiness?

How should women interpret this message? "Don't eat, but eat?" or "Eat, but don't gain weight?" or "Eat, but be on a continuous diet?" This is confusing, but it is also the message that is relayed to women on a daily basis in numerous advertisements.

Ask the girls the following questions:

- Does this message seem confusing? Why?
- Is it hard to understand and interpret this sort of message?

- What does it mean to diet?
- Can dieting harm your body? How?
- What food do you like to eat?
- What food is fun to eat?
- What food is good for your body and keeps you healthy?

Caution: Avoid using words such as "good," "bad," or "junk" when referring to food. Also, avoid discussing the fat, sugar, caloric, and carbohydrate content of various foods. Let the girls state any foods they like without judgment. If someone says "I like chocolate chip cookies," you might respond by saying, "Yes, I like those, too." This will send the message that food is food and no food is off limits; food is *not* good or bad. Sending a message that some foods are good or bad can begin the dangerous cycle of dieting.

Spend a few minutes going over the food pyramid (Appendix D). Ask the following questions:

- Have you seen this before?
- What is the purpose of the food pyramid?

BREAK (10 minutes)

COMPUTER LAB (35 Minutes) Introduce the group to the Nutrition Café located at http://www.exhibits.pacsci.org/nutrition and to Nutrition Explorations found at http://www.nutritionexplorations.org. Both are websites that talk about nutrition and have games the girls can play to increase their knowledge about eating healthy.

CLOSURE (5 minutes) Using the koosh ball, ask the girls to discuss the slogan "Scales are for fish."

- What do you think this means?
- How can scales (or weighing often) be harmful?

A homework assignment will be given. The girls will be asked to think of and write down 10 snacks that are good for their bodies. They will also be encouraged to continue as Watchdogs.

The Processing Questions

The leader will be able to ascertain if the objectives were met by listening to the girls' comments during closure.

SESSION 4: COPING WITH STRESS, PART I

The Focus

The focus of this session will be the Nonspecific Life Stress model. This model's focus is to reduce stress, to decrease risks for emotional disorders, and to increase self-esteem. The session will focus on stress, its causes, and coping strategies. The PEER model will also be used; the girls will be the authorities on stressors in their lives.

The Objectives

The objectives in this session are:

- to increase knowledge about stress;
- to help the girls identify stressful situations;
- to assist them in recognizing triggers;
- to help them find coping alternatives.

The Behavioral Outcomes

The girls will learn about stress and how it impacts their lives. They will learn how to identify stress and gain an understanding about things that trigger their stressor. Finally, they will learn how to cope with stress.

The Activities

GREETINGS (5 minutes) Instruct the girls that when the koosh ball is tossed to them, they are to share at least 2 healthy snacks from their list of 10 with the group.

BRAINSTORM (15 minutes) Have the girls sit in a semicircle and ask them to identify stressful situations in their lives. You and the cofacilitators will make a list on the board of all the situations, events, places, and so on the girls recognize as stressful (e.g., school, history class, family life, doctor visits, etc.).

SUBGROUP ACTIVITY (20 minutes) Put the girls in four groups of five and ask them to continue to brainstorm and compile a list of what the group considers to be their top five stressful situations.

BREAK (10 minutes) Snack time!

COMPUTER LAB (30 minutes) The girls will interact on several different websites to learn more about the causes and effects of stress and the steps to take when they are feeling stressed (Appendix E). The *4 Girls Health* website is a good place to get started. The section entitled "Mind Over Matters" provides information about stress in a girl-friendly way. The site also provides a "Stress Map Scale" on which the girls can answer a few questions to determine their current stress level.

You will then ask the girls to pose a question about stress. The girls can then go to the *Just 4 Girls* website and "Ask Dr. M" a question related to stress (Appendix E). During the next week, watch for a response to be posted to the site, so you can show the girls.

After they have posted their question, guide them to the *girls inc.* website and have them take the quiz titled "What is your Coping Style?" and then look at the "Stress Busters" page (Appendix E). These websites will provide the girls with insight into their physiological responses to stress and ways to cope with stress. You will secure the information they have accumulated for the next session.

CLOSURE (10 minutes) Using the koosh ball, ask the girls to state one thing they learned about stress.

The Processing Questions

The group leader will be able to ascertain what the girls learned about stress by attending to their responses during closure.

SESSION 5: COPING WITH STRESS, PART II

The Focus

The focus of this session will again be the Nonspecific Life Stress model and the PEER model and will continue to focus on the effects of stress and ways to cope with stress.

The Objectives

The goals in this session are:

- to educate the girls about the physiological and behavioral changes induced by stress;
- to identify helpful stress-coping strategies;
- to practice stress-coping strategies.

The Behavioral Outcomes

The girls will have a better understanding about the effects of stress on their bodies. They will also gain a repertoire of ways to cope with stress.

The Activities

GREETINGS (5 minutes) Ask the girls to share one positive thing that happened to them today.

COMPUTER LAB (35 minutes) Distribute the information about stress the girls found on the Internet during the previous session. Ask the girls to create a fact sheet about how to cope with stressors in their lives from the information they learned from the previous session. The title should be "Coping with Stress." The girls will meet in the same subgroups as the previous day and work on the computers creating their fact sheets. You and the cofacilitators will assist the girls in this endeavor. If time permits, the girls can go on the *KidsHealth* website, the *Club Girl Tech* website, or on the *Girl Zone* website to learn more about emotions and stress (Appendix E). The girls will be asked to decide on one coping strategy they will try the next time they feel stressed. Then, have them think of three more coping resources they would be willing to try. Give them the pledge sheet (Appendix E) and ask them to complete the form and sign it. They will keep this sheet to remind them to try a coping strategy the next time they feel stressed.

BREAK (10 minutes) During break, the cofacilitator will make copies of the girls' fact sheets for all the girls to have a copy.

CLASSROOM (25 minutes) Prearrange for a school or community nurse to join the group and take blood pressures and heart rates of those girls who volunteer. Ask the nurse to talk to the girls about the physiological aspects of stress, things that trigger stress, and ways they can cope with stress (i.e., exercise, a proper diet, relaxation techniques, etc.). If the nurse provides examples of coping strategies, allow time for the girls to practice the techniques and ask questions. The girls will each receive a copy of their fact sheets.

MEDITATION AND CLOSING (15 minutes) You will teach the girls about the benefits of meditation, introduce them to one simple breathing technique, and guide them through a meditation exercise they can use during times of increased stress (Appendix E). You can end the session after the meditation exercise.

The Processing Questions

You should be able to ascertain the amount of information the girls have processed by looking at the fact sheets and by reading their pledges to try a coping strategy.

SESSION 6: BODY IMAGE

The Focus

The focus of this session will be based on the Disorder-Specific Continuity model and the Feminist model, and will focus on the concept of body image. The girls will have an opportunity to learn about their own unique body image.

The Objectives

The objectives for this session are:

- to become sensitive to factors that influence body image;
- to help create positive body images;
- to increase self-esteem;
- to increase acceptance of a wide range of body weights and shapes.

The Behavioral Outcomes

The girls will learn that although the media usually present only one body shape, the "V" shape, other body shapes are more common (the hourglass and the pear shape) and all body shapes are acceptable. They will get a visual representation of how they and their group members view their bodies. They will also discuss their feelings and concerns about their appearance.

The Activities

GREETINGS (3 minutes) Greet the girls and ask them to share with the class the coping strategy they pledge to try the next time they feel stressed.

BODY IMAGE ACTIVITY (15 minutes) This is an activity adapted from a workshop activity sponsored by the Renfrew Center of Florida. You will need to obtain paper in advance for this activity. Large sheets or rolls of poster paper taped together will work for this exercise. Give each girl a large piece of paper—larger in height and width than the girl herself. Pair each girl with one other group member. Ask each girl to draw a life-size outline of her body on the paper. This will be her perception of her body shape (how she views her figure in her mind's eye). After the girls complete this task, ask one girl of each pair to lie inside the outline and have her partner trace her actual body size. Using a different color marker may help to more clearly distinguish between the two. Continue this exercise until all girls have had their actual body size traced over their perceived body shape.

GROUP DISCUSSION (22 minutes) Take time to discuss the difference between their actual size (the traced body shape) and their perceived size (the drawn outline of their bodies). Caution: Be careful not to make judgments about how the girls drew the outline of their bodies, regardless of whether the body image in their mind's eye is larger or smaller than their actual body size. You may have girls that are beginning the stages of puberty and are rounder than other girls. You may have girls in the group who are overweight. Reassure the girls there are no right or wrong drawings. The exercise is to help them learn to view their bodies at their actual size and accept all sizes and differences among people. Ask the girls several questions:

- Was there a difference in how you drew your body and the actual size of your body?

- If so, why do you think this difference occured?
- Do you feel most women would draw their bodies larger or smaller than they actually are?

Spend time discussing Cindy Jackson (see Appendix F). Ask the girls the following questions:

- What are the pros and cons of cosmetic surgery?
- Why do you suppose women permanently alter their bodies?
- When can plastic surgery be positive? (See Appendix F for additional questions.)

Spend time discussing Ruby (Appendix B); Armi Kuusela, Miss Universe 1952; and Linda Bement, Miss Universe 1960 (images of Kuusela and Bement can be found at www.pageant.com/universe97/index.html). Ask the girls the following questions:

- What do you think of Ruby's size?
- What do you think about the caption, "There are 3 billion women who don't look like supermodels and only 8 who do"?
- What do you think of Armi Kuusela's and Linda Bement's sizes?
- Does this size seem realistic?
- Do you know women who are this size?

This is a good place to discuss developmental issues with the girls. You will want to explain to them that as their bodies mature, it is natural and healthy for them to become rounder. It means they are becoming women! It is a time to celebrate!

BREAK (10 minutes) Snack time!

FISHBOWL AND TALKING STICK (35 minutes) This is an activity adapted from Girls in the '90s (Friedman, 1998). You and the cofacilitators will arrange the chairs into two circles—one inside the other. The inside circle will consist of 5 chairs and the outside circle will contain 20 chairs. The koosh ball will be used like a talking stick (a custom of the American Indians). The girls are already familiar with the concept of the koosh ball indicating that only the person holding it may speak; in addition, she may speak as long as she wants without interruption; however, you should reiterate this. Have the girls take a seat, with five girls sitting in the inner circle and the remaining girls taking seats in the outer circle. Explain to the girls that only the girls in the inner circle will speak and after speaking once, the girl will leave the inner circle and another girl in the outer circle will enter the inner circle to take her place. Questions will be asked to stimulate thought about body image concerns; the girls in the inner circle will discuss the questions. Allow at least four or five girls to answer and discuss each question. You may also wish to have the cofacilitators sit in the inner circle to help get things started.

These are the questions *(from the Chatelaine website at http://www.chate laine.com)*:

- What did you find interesting about the body image activity?
- What do the words fat and thin mean?
- What does a healthy body look like?—Which do you want? A strong body? A beautiful body?
- Do you think there are different types of beauty?
- What do you feel when you see pictures of models?
- What makes you forget about your appearance?
- Why would some cultures prize bigger women?
- If you ever feel fat or unattractive, what is really going on?
- The last time you felt that way, what had just happened?
- What is it like to be a girl these days?

CLOSURE (5 minutes) Use the koosh ball one last time and ask each girl to say one thing that makes her feel good about herself. The girls will again be asked to remind their parents about attending the last session.

The Processing Questions

You should be able to assess the girls' understanding of body image during the fishbowl activity.

SESSION 7: PUTTING IT ALL TOGETHER

The Focus

This session will be from the PEER model approach and will focus on helping the girls connect all they have learned from the previous session's topics.

The Objectives

The objectives in this session are:

- to recap what the girls have learned about coping with stress;
- to review what the girls have learned about media messages;
- to review what the girls have learned about food and nutrition;
- to reiterate the message about positive body image.

The Behavioral Outcomes

The girls will get a good review of the last six sessions, helping them integrate all the information they have heard. The girls will see that by applying what they have learned they will live healthier lives and avoid noxious agents that could lead to disorders.

The Activities

GREETING (5 minutes) Ask the girls to state one thing they have learned during the past six sessions.

GROUP DISCUSSION (20 minutes) Have the girls sit in a circle and ask them the following questions:

- What do we sometimes do when we get really stressed out?
- Do we make healthy choices when we get really stressed?
- Why is it important to manage stress?
- When we see really thin models on TV or in magazines, do we sometimes feel bad that we don't look like they do?
- Do the media sometimes send a message that there is only one body type that is beautiful?
- What can we do to stop starvation imagery in the media?

ACTIVITY (15 minutes) This activity and its questions are from Jennifer O'Dea's "New Self-Esteem Approach" (2001). Ask one of the girls in the class to draw a person on the board. Then ask the girls the following questions:

- What makes up a person?
- What makes us the same?

- What makes us different?
- What makes us unique?
- What does acceptance mean?
- Why is it important to accept others that are different from us?

BREAK (10 minutes)

ACTIVITY (25 minutes) Have the girls spend time on several websites to find information about the topics they have discussed over the past six sessions. *4 Girls Health* has wonderful information in the section about "You Are What You Eat" and "Fit for Life." *KidsHealth* also provides great information on "Staying Healthy" and has games the girls can play. *Club Girl Tech* has games to play, and *girls inc.* has a "Know Your Emotions" section and "The Girls Bill of Rights" that are both quite empowering for girls (Appendix E). The girls may wish to print a copy of the Girls Bill of Rights, decorate it, and bring it home to hang in their bedrooms.

CLOSURE (15 minutes) Ask the girls to discuss what they learned from the websites.

The Processing Questions

You should be able to determine how well the girls processed the information from previous sessions by listening to their comments during closure.

SESSION 8: *THE MORE YOU KNOW*

The Focus

This session's focus will be from the feminist model. (The slogan for this session is from NBC's Public Service Announcement series.) The girls will again become advocates for change.

The Objectives

The goals in this session are:

- to make changes in the social environment;
- to help girls apply the knowledge they have learned in a creative manner.

The Behavioral Outcomes

The girls will apply the information they have learned in a creative way, thus encouraging critical thinking skills. They will also be empowered by being involved in a social change activity.

The Activities

GREETINGS (3 minutes) Ask the girls if they have any questions about the previous sessions. You and the cofacilitators will share information from the e-mail inquiries that have received responses.

PUBLIC SERVICE ANNOUNCEMENT (35 minutes) Have the girls view *The More You Know* website and read scripts from previous public service announcements (PSAs) (Appendix H). Ask them questions about PSAs, such as:

- What is a PSA?
- Why do television stations like NBC run PSAs?
- Do you think people are affected by PSAs?

Ask the girls to brainstorm ideas for future *The More You Know* series dealing with the topics of media literacy, dieting and nutrition, body image, and stress, discussed in the past sessions. Divide the girls into four groups of five, give them a copy of the scripts from previous programs (Appendix H), and ask them to come up with a public service announcement for NBC's *The More You Know*. Each subgroup will write a script and determine who would be the best spokesperson. This spokesperson might be a favorite actor, singer, author, athlete, or public figure.

BREAK (10 minutes)

PUBLIC SERVICE ANNOUNCEMENT (15 minutes) Give the girls more time to finish their PSAs and then ask each group to share it with the class. Ask them a few questions, such as:

- Why might NBC be reluctant to air messages against dieting?
- Who advertises on television?
- Would NBC be reluctant to speak out against dieting if their main advertiser is a dieting company?

COMPUTER LAB (15 minutes) Have the girls e-mail NBC their scripts for *The More You Know* series (Appendix H). You and the cofacilitators will check e-mail on a daily basis to see if there has been a response.

CLOSURE (10 minutes) Ask the girls two final processing questions.

The Processing Questions

- What have you learned from today's session?
- Can the media be a positive force in society?

SESSION 9: BECOMING THE TEACHER

The Focus

The approach will be the PEER model. The girls will become the authorities by imparting information they have learned.

The Objectives

The objectives in this session are:

- to reinforce the information the girls have learned;
- to empower the girls by having them take the role of the authority.

The Behavioral Outcomes

The girls will become empowered by taking on the role of teacher. By reviewing the information presented in the past two weeks, the girls will gain a better understanding of how it all ties together.

The Activities

GREETINGS (5 minutes) Ask the girls to tell the group the one thing they would like their parents to know about what they have learned during the past weeks.

SUBGROUPS (35 minutes) Assemble the girls in four groups of five and ask each group to choose a topic (e.g., dieting, body image, media messages, or stress). Ask each group to brainstorm for a few minutes to decide what information they would like their parents to know about the specific topic they have chosen. From there, they are to plan a short skit or presentation (possibly something related to *The More You Know* program) for their parents. It should be informational and entertaining. You and the cofacilitators will need to assist and guide the groups through this process.

BREAK (10 minutes)

SUBGROUPS (20 minutes) Have the girls reconvene in their groups and continue planning their brief skits/presentations to the parents. The cofacilitators can copy any handouts the girls want to provide to the parents before the next session.

CLOSURE (20 minutes) Ask the girls to form one circle; it is time to discuss the topic of termination. Ask the girls to discuss their feelings about no longer meeting with the group. Make sure you have at least 20 minutes to discuss termination. (Please note: It would be easy to get caught up in skit preparation and forgo this discussion; however, this is an important part of the process and the girls need time to define and discuss their feelings. Some girls might feel sad or even stressed that the group is disbanding. They need to have some closure from the leader and other members.) The discussion should also center on growth and a summary of what was learned during the past two weeks.

The Processing Questions

- How do you feel about leaving the group?
- What have you learned that could improve your life?

SESSION 10: PARENTAL INVOLVEMENT

The Focus

The focus of this session will be to allow the girls to say good-bye to one another. They will be given time to process their feelings about termination and to summarize what they have learned. They will also have the opportunity to demonstrate what they have learned by presenting information to their parents. This session will use the PEER model.

The Objectives

The goals in this session are:

- to empower the girls by allowing them to be the authorities;
- to provide the girls with an opportunity to say good-bye.

The Behavioral Outcomes

The girls will impart information and demonstrate what they have learned. They will also say good-bye.

The Activities

SUBGROUPS (17 minutes) The girls will be given an opportunity to make any final preparations to their skits/presentations.

GROUP DISCUSSION (15 minutes) Facilitate a group discussion, summarizing what has been learned and allowing the girls to reflect on their experience.

POSTTEST (8 minutes) The girls will be asked to complete the Children's Version of the Eating Attitudes Test (Appendix A). The cofacilitators will be asked to complete a questionnaire evaluating the group leader (Appendix A).

BREAK (10 minutes)

WELCOME PARENTS (5 minutes) You and the cofacilitators will conduct introductions and welcome the parents and guardians to the final session. Explain to the parents that the girls have prepared some presentations for them about different issues. Introduce each subgroup in turn.

SKITS/PRESENTATIONS (25 minutes) Each subgroup will present its skit or presentation to the audience.

CLOSURE (10 minutes) Thank the parents or guardians for joining the group, answer any questions the parents might have, provide them with a few handouts (Appendix I), and invite them to lunch (if you are going to have a luncheon).

Appendix A

Forms and Questionnaires

PERMISSION FORM

I, _____, give permission for
my daughter, _____, to participate in
Body Armor. I understand that the group's ultimate goal is the prevention of
eating disorders. I also understand that my daughter will learn about potentially destructive media messages and starvation imagery that promotes dieting behavior, which can result in a negative body image. My daughter will
learn how to cope with stress, and she will learn that dieting is unhealthy. She
will also explore how women can be negatively depicted in the media and
how to become an activist against such messages.

_____   _____
          Date   Parent or Guardian's Signature

GOALS AND OBJECTIVES OF THE
BODY ARMOR PREVENTION PROGRAM

1. To reduce the negative influential effects of the media by promoting critical thinking.
2. To make changes in the social environment regarding how women are
   presented in the media.
3. To provide information about dieting and nutrition.
4. To assist the girls in recognizing triggers for stress and to develop coping
   strategies for stress.
5. To practice stress-coping strategies.
6. To become sensitive to factors that influence body image and to help create positive body image.
7. To increase acceptance of a wide range of body weights and shapes.

CONFIDENTIALITY

- I understand that information shared in a group setting is to remain confidential (private).
- I can share information I learn in the group with my friends and family, but I understand that I cannot talk about the other girls and the things they say in the group to other people.
- I also understand that if I discuss harming myself or if I discuss being harmed by someone else, the group leader will share this information with my parents and/or the appropriate authorities.
- I understand that if I tell the group leader or cofacilitator that a child or an elderly person I know is being harmed, the group leader or cofacilitator will need to report this information to the proper authorities.
- I understand that the group leader cannot ensure confidentiality. This means the group leader has little control over making sure no one discusses private information outside of the group. However, all girls participating in the group will be asked to sign this form.

_____   _____
            Signature   Date

QUESTIONNAIRE FOR PARENT OR GUARDIAN

1. I am scared about being overweight.
    Always   Very Often   Often   Sometimes   Rarely   Never

2. I am aware of the fat and/or calorie content in foods that I eat.
    Always   Very Often   Often   Sometimes   Rarely   Never

3. I try to stay away from foods such as breads, potatoes, and rice.
    Always   Very Often   Often   Sometimes   Rarely   Never

4. I feel very guilty after eating.
    Always   Very Often   Often   Sometimes   Rarely   Never

5. I think a lot about wanting to be thinner.
    Always   Very Often   Often   Sometimes   Rarely   Never

6. I eat diet foods.
    Always   Very Often   Often   Sometimes   Rarely   Never

7. I give too much time and thought to food.
    Always   Very Often   Often   Sometimes   Rarely   Never

8. I stay away from foods with sugar in them.
    Always   Very Often   Often   Sometimes   Rarely   Never

9. I am interested in serving as a cofacilitator of this prevention group.
    Yes_____ No_____ Maybe_____

10. I am currently on a diet.
    Yes_____ No_____ If yes, describe diet: _____
    _____
    _____
    _____

11. I am interested in learning more about my body image and weight
    prejudices.
    Yes_____ No_____

12. (If you answered yes to question 10, please answer question 12.)
    I am willing to stop dieting while cofacilitating this group.
    Yes_____ No_____

CHILDREN'S VERSION OF THE EATING ATTITUDES TEST

Instructions: Please place an X under the word that best applies to the following statements.

Sample item: I like to eat vegetables.
   Always   Very Often   Often   Sometimes   Rarely   Never

1. I am scared about being overweight.
    Always   Very Often   Often   Sometimes   Rarely   Never

2. I stay away from eating when I am hungry.
    Always   Very Often   Often   Sometimes   Rarely   Never

3. I think about food a lot of the time.
    Always   Very Often   Often   Sometimes   Rarely   Never

4. I have gone on eating binges where I feel that I might not be able to stop.
    Always   Very Often   Often   Sometimes   Rarely   Never

5. I cut my food into small pieces.
    Always   Very Often   Often   Sometimes   Rarely   Never

6. I am aware of the energy (calorie) content in foods that I eat.
    Always   Very Often   Often   Sometimes   Rarely   Never

7. I try to stay away from foods such as breads, potatoes, and rice.
    Always   Very Often   Often   Sometimes   Rarely   Never

8. I feel that others would like me to eat more.
    Always   Very Often   Often   Sometimes   Rarely   Never

9. I vomit after I have eaten.
    Always   Very Often   Often   Sometimes   Rarely   Never

10. I feel very guilty after eating.
    Always   Very Often   Often   Sometimes   Rarely   Never

11. I think a lot about wanting to be thinner.
    Always   Very Often   Often   Sometimes   Rarely   Never

12. I think about burning up energy (calories) when I exercise.
    Always   Very Often   Often   Sometimes   Rarely   Never

13.   Other people think I am too thin.
      Always   Very Often   Often   Sometimes   Rarely   Never

14.   I think a lot about having fat on my body.
      Always   Very Often   Often   Sometimes   Rarely   Never

15.   I take longer than others to eat my meals.
      Always   Very Often   Often   Sometimes   Rarely   Never

16.   I stay away from foods with sugar in them.
      Always   Very Often   Often   Sometimes   Rarely   Never

17.   I eat diet foods.
      Always   Very Often   Often   Sometimes   Rarely   Never

18.   I think that food controls my life.
      Always   Very Often   Often   Sometimes   Rarely   Never

19.   I can show self-control around food.
      Always   Very Often   Often   Sometimes   Rarely   Never

20.   I feel that others pressure me to eat.
      Always   Very Often   Often   Sometimes   Rarely   Never

21.   I give too much time and thought to food.
      Always   Very Often   Often   Sometimes   Rarely   Never

22.   I feel uncomfortable after eating sweets.
      Always   Very Often   Often   Sometimes   Rarely   Never

23.   I have been dieting.
      Always   Very Often   Often   Sometimes   Rarely   Never

24.   I like my stomach to be empty.
      Always   Very Often   Often   Sometimes   Rarely   Never

25.   I enjoy trying new rich foods.
      Always   Very Often   Often   Sometimes   Rarely   Never

26.   I have the urge to vomit after eating.
      Always   Very Often   Often   Sometimes   Rarely   Never

Source: M. J. Maloney, 1988. Reliability testing of the Children's Version of the Eating Attitudes Test, *Journal of the American Academy of Child and Adolescent Psychiatry*, *27* (pp. 542–543). Reprinted with permission.

COFACILITATOR EVALUATION OF THE GROUP LEADER

This evaluation provides you with an opportunity to express your views about the effectiveness of the group leader. Your answers are important because they will help the group leader improve her leadership skills and enhance the overall psychoeducational program.

Please answer using the following scale:

Strongly Agree	1
Agree	2
Undecided	3
Disagree	4
Strongly Disagree	5

_____ 1. The group leader appears to have a broad knowledge of the subject matter.

_____ 2. The group sessions were well organized and followed the stated objectives of the group manual.

_____ 3. The group sessions began on time.

_____ 4. The group sessions ended on time.

_____ 5. The group leader maintained member interest by making the sessions challenging.

_____ 6. The group leader communicated the information clearly.

_____ 7. The group leader treated all members with dignity and respect.

_____ 8. The group leader had a strong rapport with the group members.

_____ 9. The group members responded favorably to the group leader.

_____10. The use of multimedia greatly enhanced the sessions and helped the group members better understand the information.

_____11. The group leader used active listening (the ability to hear, understand, and communicate this understanding).

_____12. The group leader effectively used questioning (the ability to use questions to stimulate thought and action, and to avoid a question/answer pattern of interaction between the leader and member).

_____13. The group leader helped members clarify their own goals and take the steps to reach them.

_____14. The group leader gave information to the members in such a way that they can use it to make constructive behavior changes.

_____15. The group leader demonstrated to members desired behaviors that can be practiced both during and after group sessions.

_____16. The group leader suggested to members specific activities that they could practice both in and out of group to develop new behaviors.

_____17. The group leader was inventive and creative.

_____18. The group leader communicated an attitude of acceptance.

_____19. The group leader demonstrated an attitude of genuine caring, warmth, and concern for the members.

_____20. The group leader created a climate that encouraged members to continue working after sessions.

Note: Questions 11–20 are from the *Evaluation Form of Group Leader Skills* created by Dr. Richard Maeder, Retired Associate Professor of Counselor Education, Florida Atlantic University.

YOU ARE INVITED!

Please join us on _____ from _____ for a
                          DATE   TIME
program presented by your daughter and the other girls participating in the
Body Armor Program. The girls have prepared a brief presentation to help
you understand what they have learned while participating in the prevention
program. The program is also designed to help you better understand the risk
factors for developing an eating disorder and will provide you with specific
strategies you can use to help prevent them.

The program will be held at   _____
                                                              LOCATION

We look forward to seeing you!

Appendix B

TAKING A CLOSER LOOK

There are 3 billion women who don't look like supermodels and only 8 who do. (Image of Ruby reprinted with permission from the Body Shop. http://www.thebodyshop.com.)

ABOUT-FACE: HTTP://WWW.ABOUT-FACE.ORG

Before looking at the following advertisements, have a brief discussion about the ads you are about to view. (As the leader, view the ads in advance; you may want to find additional ads to demonstrate the following points.) Ask the girls to pay attention to three things:

1. Ask them to look for ads that dismember or crop the body of a woman. "Women's bodies without heads, faces or feet lead us to believe that all that truly matters about a woman lies between her neck and her knees." (Quote from the About-Face website at http://www.about-face.org/goo/newten/4/six.shtml.)
2. Ask them to look for ads that suggest that a woman's appearance must be flawless. "The perfect woman is not human; she is a shell representing a female form." (Quote from the About-Face website at http://www.about-face.org/goo/newten/4/five.shtml.)
3. Ask them to view how the women are positioned. "People in charge of their own lives typically stand up straight. . . . In contrast, the bending of the body conveys unpreparedness and submissiveness." (Quote from the About-Face website at http://www.about-face. org/goo/newten/4/three.shtml.)

Now, the girls are ready to view the ads.

Decoding Media Messages From the About-Face Website's Gallery of Offenders

Gucci's ad clearly depicts concept #1—body chopping; see http://www. about-face.org/goo/newten/4/six.shtml.

Moschino's ad demonstrates concept #2—the perfect Barbie Doll; see http://www.about-face.org/goo/newten/4/five.shtml.

Christian Dior's perfume ad is quite offensive to women and illustrates concept #3—submissiveness; see http://www.about-face.org/goo/newten/4/three.shtml.

In addition, you may want to allow the girls to look through fashion magazines and find additional examples of ads that are particularly offensive to women.

From the About-Face Website's Gallery of Winners

In contrast to the Gallery of Offenders, many ads reflect positive images of women. Have the girls view the following ads and ask them questions about each ad.

The Body Shop sponsored a self-esteem campaign and used Ruby, a doll, to depict the real woman. The ad reads, "There are 3 billion women who don't look like supermodels and only 8 who do." Why is this ad in the Gallery of Winners? What do you think about Ruby's size? Do you think this ad helps women feel better about their bodies? http://www.about-face.org/gow/newten/1/index.shtml.

This ad by Panasonic shows a girl spattered in mud with a huge smile on her face. The ad reads, "Mud, Sweat, & Tunes." What makes this ad a winner? Does the girl appear to be in charge? Powerful? How do you feel when you see this ad? http://www.about-face.org/gow/newten/1/eight.shtml.

This Chic jeans ad shows all different types of women, yet all are beautiful. There are young and old women, Black and White women, short and tall women. Why is this ad a winner? Do you like this ad? http://www.about-face.org/gow/newten/3/six.shtml.

The girls can look through magazines and find ads that reflect women in a positive way.

BREAKING-THE-CODE ACTIVITY

Directions: Connect the numbers from #1 to #40. You have one minute.

1   39

                                      25

                                                                          18

37   9   2   20

                              3   6

          27   8   28

                      5

                                              10

          7   15   12   14

                              11   38

          33   34   26

13   32   24

                      19   36

17   40   4

          23   21   30

31   29   22

          35   16

Appendix C

HAVING A VOICE

View letters to companies and submission guidelines at http://www.about-face.org/yv/.

National Eating Disorders WebPages; see   http://www.nationaleating disorders.org.

Letters of Protest and Praise; see http://www.nationaleatingdisorders.org/p.asp?WebPage_ID=336.

Becoming a Media Watchdog Program; see http://www.nationaleating disorder.org/p.asp?WebPage_ID=300.

Appendix D

SCALES ARE FOR FISH

USDA FOOD GUIDE PYRAMID

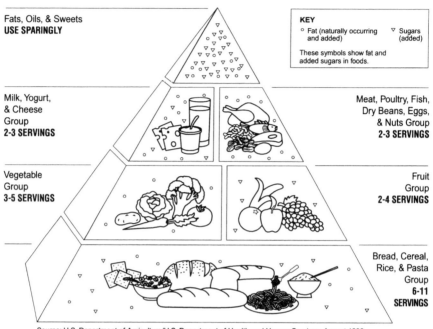

Source: U.S. Department of Agriculture/U.S. Department of Health and Human Services, August 1992

Use the Food Guide Pyramid to help you eat better every day...the Dietary Guidelines way. Start with plenty of Breads, Cereals, Rice, and Pasta; Vegetables; and Fruits. Add two to three servings from the Milk group and two to three servings from the Meat group.

Each of these food groups provides some, but not all, of the nutrients you need. No one food group is more important than another—for good health you need them all. Go easy on fats, oils, and sweets, the foods in the small tip of the Pyramid.

Internet sources for Food Guide Pyramid: http://www.nal.usda.gov:8001/py/pmap.htm; http://www.eatsmart.org/; and http://www.kidfood.org/f_pyramid/pyramid.html.

The girls can learn about food at http://www.kidfood.org.

See also Food Fun Activities at http://www.kidfood.org/kf_cyber.html.

More Food Fun Activities at http://www.exhibits.pacsci.org/nutrition/.

Appendix E

COPING WITH STRESS

WEBSITES FOR SESSION 4: COPING WITH STRESS, PART I

4 Girls Health: http://www.4girls.gov

Mind Over Matters at http://www.4girls.gov/mind

Stress map scales at http://www.4girls.gov/mind/scales.htm

The stress model at http://www.4girls.gov/mind/model.htm

girls inc.: http://www.girlsinc.org/gc/

What is your coping style? Quiz at http://www.girlsinc.org/gc/ page.php?id=1.2.4

Stress Busters at http://www.girlsinc.org/gc/page.php?id=1.2.5

Just 4 Girls: http://jfg.girlscouts.org/mainmenu/main.html

Dear Dr. M at http://jfg.girlscouts.org/Talk/talk.htm

WEBSITES FOR SESSION 5: COPING WITH STRESS, PART II

Club Girl Tech: http://www.girltech.com/home.cfm

Encarta: http://encarta.msn.com/encnet/refpages/artcenter.aspx

Girl Zone: http://girlzone.com/index.html

Don't Stress Out: You Can Deal With It. Here's How. at http:// www.girlzone.com/insideout/Stress_io.html

KidsHealth: http://kidshealth.org/kid/index.jsp

The Story on Stress at http://kidshealth.org/kid/feeling/emotion/ stress.html

Talking About Your Feelings at http://kidshealth.org/kid/feeling/ thought/talk_feelings.html

MY PLEDGE

The next time I feel stressed, I pledge to try one of the following coping strategies to help reduce the stress.

#1 Coping Strategy

_____

#2 Coping Strategy

_____

#3 Coping Strategy

_____

#4 Coping Strategy

_____

Sign _____

Date _____

BREATHING AND MEDITATION EXERCISES

Before you begin, explain to the girls that you want them to try to do a visual meditation. Explain to them that visual meditation is a way to help them create relaxing pictures in their minds, similar to what happens when they read a book or listen to music. The purpose of the meditation is to help them relax and reduce stress.

Ask them to get comfortable in their chairs and close their eyes. Lower the shades in the classroom and dim the lights. You may also wish to play some relaxing music quietly.

First, you will teach the girls a breathing exercise that is a modified version of an exercise that appears in *The Anxiety & Phobia Workbook* (Bourne, 1995) to help them begin the relaxation process. After the breathing exercise, take the girls on a visual meditation journey. Slowly and softly read the following script.

Before we begin, take several deep breaths. Breath in through your nose and while you do so, I want you to count slowly to five—1 . . . 2 . . . 3 . . . 4 . . . 5. Now, hold the breath for a count of five—1 . . . 2 . . . 3 . . . 4 . . . 5. Slowly release the breath through your mouth while counting to five—1 . . . 2 . . . 3 . . . 4 . . . 5. Let's try this again. This time, make sure the air you inhale is filling your entire abdomen. (You should demonstrate—your ribs and stomach area should expand.) Begin inhaling through your nose while counting to five. (Repeat this sequence.) Good; let's do this one more time. (Repeat the sequence.)

Now, with your eyes closed, begin by imagining a large wall with a beautifully decorated gate. The wall is made of red brick and has bright green vines and brilliant yellow honeysuckle flowers draped all along it. The gate is the brightest blue color you have ever seen and is wedged open slightly, inviting you to enter. You walk to the gate and give it a gentle push. It swings open easily and you step inside.

You have entered a lovely garden with trees and grass and bushes. There are flowers everywhere. You hear birds chirping and see butterflies flying from flower to flower. The sun is warm on your skin and a slight breeze cools the air. As you step inside, your entire body feels that this is a place of serenity and peace and that everything in this garden loves you and welcomes you.

As you look around, you see that every flower in this garden is the color red. The red is the most vibrant, beautiful red color you have ever seen. The red flowers are all different shapes and sizes and when you look in front of you, you are surprised to see a red flower shaped like a heart. As you take a deep breath, you smell the most amazing aroma. It smells clean and fresh. You notice an inviting swing made out of wicker. The wicker swing has red flowers intertwined in it and has a welcoming overstuffed red pillow that invites you to come sit and relax. The swing is encircled by beautiful rocks that you sense will protect whoever sits within the circle. You walk to the wicker swing, sit, and gaze at the red flowers.

You begin to feel that the red flowers are trying to give you something. You realize that the red flowers are filled with courage and want to share that courage with you. You reach out and touch a red flower. The courage begins traveling from your fingers to your arms. You feel it filling your body, and your toes begin to tingle with the power of courage. Now you feel the courage of the red flowers enter your legs (pause), your stomach (pause), your heart (pause), your back (pause), your shoulders (pause), your neck (pause), your face (pause), and your entire head. The courage provided to you by the red flowers is a wonderful tingling sensation in your body. You inhale deeply and can feel the courage flowing throughout your body.

As you sit and breathe in the courage the red flowers are offering you, you notice another large gate. It is the brightest yellow you have ever seen and it is slightly open, beckoning you to enter. You slowly rise from the wicker swing and walk over to the yellow gate. You push the gate, and it opens easily. You walk through and enter another garden with trees and bushes and grass and birds and butterflies and flowers. Your entire body feels that this, too, is a place of serenity and peace and that everything in this garden loves you and welcomes you. You know no harm can come to you here.

You are struck with awe when you notice that all the flowers are white. They are the brightest white you have ever seen. As the warm sunlight hits the flowers, you are amazed to see them sparkle as though they are filled with glitter. You notice a tree stump in the middle of the garden in the shape of a chair, and begin walking in that direction. As you make your way to the welcoming chair, you are amazed to see that some of the large, white flowers look almost like clouds in the sky. The small flowers resemble a puff of cotton with soft petals blowing in the cool breeze.

As you sit on the tree stump and gaze into the garden, you are once again struck with the sensation that the flowers want to give you something. You breathe deeply and smell an incredible aroma. It is your favorite scent. You realize that the flowers want to give you their healing powers. You reach out and touch a flower near the tree stump. You immediately feel the healing power of the white flowers traveling up your fingers and into your arms. You breathe deeply, allowing the healing powers to enter your body. This healing power expands throughout your body, making its way to your toes. As you continue to breathe in this healing power, you feel its warmth enter your legs (pause), your stomach (pause), your heart (pause), your back (pause), your shoulders (pause), your neck (pause), your face (pause), and your entire head (pause). You take several deep breaths, allowing the healing power to travel throughout your body.

You know it is time to leave the garden, but you also know you can return at any time. As you stand to go, the white flowers swaying in the wind seem to be waving good-bye to you. You can feel that they want you to return to the garden to receive the peace and the healing powers they have to offer. You slowly walk through the garden with the white flowers toward the bright yellow gate. You take one last look at the glittery white flowers and wave good-bye to them. You enter the garden with the red flowers and walk through; you linger and smell the clean, fresh aroma emitted by these flowers. Again, the flowers appear to be waving good-bye and you know they want you to come back to visit to receive the courage they have to offer you. You move toward the bright blue door and, before walking through, you take one last look at the garden with the red flowers. You again wave good-bye and then move through the blue door. You feel satisfied and peaceful and are happy that you can return to the garden any time you need peace, courage, or healing power.

When you are ready, slowly open your eyes. Take a few deep, cleansing breaths. (pause)

Allow the music to play for a few more minutes. Wait a few minutes before turning up the lights.

Appendix F

BODY IMAGE

MEET CINDY JACKSON

At the age of 33, Cindy Jackson began a total body transformation and "embarked on a marathon of surgery." To date, she has had 28 surgeries. In one interview she commented, "Despite being put ahead a year at school and later becoming a member of Mensa—the high-IQ society—I was always made to feel bad about myself because of the way I looked" (Cindy Jackson website: http://www.cindyjackson.com).

After reading this quote to the girls, ask them the following questions:

- Have you ever felt this way?
- When have you felt this way?
- How does our society define beauty?
- Do most people seem to fit society's idea of beauty?
- Is beauty just on the outside of a person?

You may wish to show before-and-after pictures of Ms. Jackson. (Before and after photos can be viewed at http://www.cindyjackson.com) Ask the girls the following questions:

- Do you often feel there is something about your body that you would like to change?
- What do you like about your body?
- What can your body do (e.g., play tennis, jump rope, swim, dance, etc.)?
- Do you ever think how unique and special your body is? If so, what is unique and special about your body?

A List of Cindy Jackson's Cosmetic Surgeries

Skin resurfacing	[3] Facelifts
Cheek Implants	Dermabrasion
Fat Transfer	Jaw line Liposuction
Chemical Peel	Cosmetic Peels
Waistline & Abdominal Liposuction	Knee Liposuction
Hair Transplant	Upper and Lower Eye Lift
Rhinoplasty [2 nose jobs]	Lip Augmentation
Cosmetic Dentistry	Chin Reduction
Semipermanent Makeup	Breast Implants
High & Inner-Thigh Liposuction	Outer Thigh Liposuction

Source: Cindy Jackson website: http://www.cindyjackson.com.

Appendix G

PUTTING IT ALL TOGETHER

ANOREXIA NERVOSA

Diagnostic criteria for anorexia nervosa from the *Diagnostic and Statistical Manual of Mental Disorders*, fourth edition, text revision (American Psychiatric Association, 2000):

A. Refusal to maintain body weight at or above a minimally normal weight for age and height;
B. Intense fear of gaining weight or becoming fat, even though underweight;
C. Disturbance in the way in which one's body weight or shape is experienced, undue influence of body weight or shape on self-evaluation, or denial of the seriousness of the current low body weight;
D. In postmenarcheal females, amenorrhea, i.e., the absence of at least three consecutive menstrual cycles. (p. 589)

BULIMIA NERVOSA

Diagnostic criteria for bulimia nervosa from the *DSM-IV-TR* (American Psychiatric Association, 2000):

A. Recurrent episodes of binge eating; an episode of binge eating is characterized by both of the following:
   1. Eating, in a discrete period of time (e.g., within a 2-hour period), an amount of food that is definitely larger than most people would eat during a similar period of time and under similar circumstances;
   2. A sense of lack of control over eating during the episode (e.g., a feeling that one cannot stop eating or control what or how much one is eating.

B. Recurrent inappropriate compensatory behavior, in order to prevent weight gain, such as self-induced vomiting; misuse of laxatives, diuretics, enemas, or other medications; fasting; or excessive exercise.
C. The binge eating and inappropriate compensatory behaviors both occur, on average, at least twice a week for 3 months.
D. Self-evaluation is unduly influenced by body shape and weight.
E. Disturbance does not occur exclusively during episodes of anorexia nervosa. (p.594)

SESSION 7: ACTIVITY INFORMATION

girls inc., Know Your Emotions at http://www.girlsinc.org/gc/page.php?id=1.2.1

Voice Your Choice: The Girls' Bill of Rights at http://www.girlsinc.org/gc/page.php?id=3.2.1

Appendix H

The More You Know

NBC's website, http://www.nbc.com/nbc/footer/tmyk/pgv_moreabout _didyouknow.shtml, provides information about the "The More You Know" campaign (the slogan is from NBC's Public Service Announcement series). This campaign has featured over 250 stars and has won numerous awards for its PSAs, including the George Foster Peabody Award, the Christopher Award, an Emmy Award, the Gracie Allen Award, the Clarion Award, the Prism Award, and the National Education Association Award for the Advancement of Learning Through Broadcasting.

The girls can review this website and the scripts and write their PSAs, naming the artist that they would like to see featured in the PSA. They will then submit them to NBC at nbcshows@nbc.com.

THE MORE YOU KNOW SCRIPTS

Teen Pregnancy

"Having a baby isn't like playing with a doll. If this were a real baby, you'd have to do these things 30 times a day for a real long time. You think you're up for it? Having a kid doesn't make you a grown-up. Waiting until you're ready does" (performed by Laura Innes from *ER*).

Teen Pregnancy

"Ok. You're a teenager and you get offered a job. You gotta work 24 hours a day and the boss is this totally helpless, demanding type who expects you to do everything. Plus, oh your personal life always comes second. You'd have to be crazy, right? Nope. You just have to have a baby. Babies are a full-time job. One you can't quit and don't get paid for. So, if you're young and not ready to work that hard—You're not ready to have a baby either" (performed by Maria Bello from *ER*).

Parental Involvement

"Kids. Gotta love 'em. There's this little four-year-old kid, lives next door to me, Mac. He keeps coming over with his little books for me to read to him. His favorite is *Green Eggs and Ham*. He's got them all memorized— knows every line. If I try to skip a page, he bites me. But that's okay. That's kids and I know that reading to a kid helps them prepare to go off to school someday—where they can bite each other for a change" (performed by David Schwimmer from *Friends*).

_____

Note: Scripts quoted from NBC's Public Service Announcement website at http://www. nbc.com/nbc/footer.tmyk/pgv_moreabout_didyouknow.shtml.

Appendix I

Resource Materials for Parents and Guardians

HANDOUTS

THE RENFREW CENTER FOUNDATION provides an abundance of excellent and free downloadable educational posters, flyers, and quizzes. This site provides a comprehensive book list for kids, for fun, for parents, for those in treatment, and so on. "Do I contribute to Another's Eating Disorder?" and "Prevention Tips for Parents" are two ideal handouts to copy and provide to parents during the last session. http://www.renfrewcenter.com/resources/index.asp#Cat9.

THE NATIONAL EATING DISORDERS ASSOCIATION has comprehensive prevention and awareness materials for $10. Their "Early Childhood Prevention Packet for Elementary School Educators" is $5. The materials contain information such as *Ten Things Parents Can Do to Help Prevent Eating Disorders*, for parents and guardians. Resources for Parents and Guardians can be purchased from: Eating Disorders Awareness and Prevention, Inc., 603 Stewart St., Suite 803, Seattle, WA 98101, 1-800-931-2237, http://www.national eatingdisorders.org/p.asp?WebPage_ID=373&Profile_ID=43.

EMPOWERING WEBSITES

Educators and parents alike will benefit from the information provided at the following websites:

CLUB GIRL TECH www.girltech.com. This website is another great place for girls; it provides games, information, and a safe place for girls to voice their opinions.

DADS AND DAUGHTERS http://www.dadsanddaughters.org/index.html. This website is a national nonprofit organization that is directed towards Dads. Its function is to education and advocate for healthy father/daughter relationships. Dads explore the current cultural messages that value girls more for their appearance than for their strengths and talents. These dads take action and have had success with their protests against negative advertisements. These successes are outlined on the site.

DAUGHTERS TOO BOOKS FOR GIRLS http://www.daughterstoo.futuresite. register.com. This site lists books that present girls in the starring role. The characters in the books are independent, intelligent, strong, courageous, creative, and assertive.

FEMINIST.COM http://www.feminist.com. Educators and parents will love this website. There are numerous articles that will spark interesting discussions. Some articles and poems are written by teens. The site also has a bookstore and inspiring quotes to explore.

GIRL POWER http://www.girlpower.gov. The U.S. Department of Health and Human Services created this website targeting girls ages 9–13 to encourage them to be healthy; to discuss issues, such as eating disorders, fitness, and so on; and to motivate girls to live life to the fullest.

GIRLS CAN DO http://www.girlscandobooks.com. This website helps parents of girls select books that encourage confidence and self-esteem. It offers a free newsletter and parents can join the feminist book club.

GIRLS INC. www.girlsinc.org. Girls inc. is a nonprofit organization that inspires all girls to be strong, smart, and bold. The organization addresses math and science education for girls, literacy, prevention, and more. There are fun activities for girls that promote health and inspire girls to be bold.

GIRL ZONE www.girlzone.com. This site allows girls to learn about their bodies, participate in contests, talk to other girls, seek advice, discuss careers and college, and much more.

KIDSHEALTH www.kidshealth.org. This website is a place for kids to go to learn about their bodies, emotions, health, growing up, and so on. There are fun games for kids to play. This site also provides information for parents and teens.

LILYPADBOOKS.COM CHILDREN'S BOOKS YOU CAN COUNT ON! http://www.lilypadbooks.com. This site promises only good books for girls and boys and lists books specifically tailored for girls.

NEW MOON PUBLISHING http://www.newmoon.org/. This site provides information about the magazine New Moon, a magazine for girls. In addition, there are products for girls, a newsletter, information about books, and a free curriculum for teachers.

EATING DISORDERS RESOURCES

ALLIANCE FOR EATING DISORDERS AWARENESS http://www.eatingdisorder info.org/. This website provides information appropriate for children and adolescents about eating disorders. It also targets parents to educate them about the dangers of eating disorders.

AMERICAN ANOREXIA/BULIMIA ASSOCIATION, INC. http://www.4woman. gov/. This site was created by the U.S. Department of Health and Human Services to provide free information to women about health-related issues. This page provides extensive information about eating disorders—risks, causes, types, treatments, and research.

ANOREXIA NERVOSA AND RELATED EATING DISORDERS, INC. (ANRED) http://www.anred.com. ANRED is a nonprofit organization. The website contains useful information such as statistics, warning signs, causes, treatment, relapse prevention, and prevention strategies for parents.

EATING DISORDER COALITION http://www.eatingdisorderscoalition.org/ index.html. This website is devoted to changing how the federal government views eating disorders, and those active in this coalition work to affect policy decisions about eating disorders as a public-health concern.

EATING DISORDER REFERRAL AND INFORMATION CENTER http://www.ed referral.com. This site is an excellent place to locate an eating disorder specialist to begin treatment. It also provides a plethora of information to educate the public about eating disorders.

EATING DISORDERS ANONYMOUS (EDA) http://www.eatingdisordersanony mous.org. EDA provides a 24/7 chat line/support group for individuals to discuss eating disorders, their hopes, struggles, and success stories with others who are also struggling for health. They also list EDA meetings in 19 states and provide other helpful information about eating-disorder treatment and recovery.

THE ELISA PROJECT http://www.theelisaproject.org. This website is somewhat of a tribute to Elisa Ruth McCall, who took her own life after struggling for years with an eating disorder. Elisa's parents created a nonprofit organization, The Elisa Project, to provide support for others struggling with eating disorders. The site provides good resource materials and some links to other good sites. Most powerful are the excerpts from Elisa's journal.

EMPOWERED KIDZ http://www.empoweredkidz.com. This is an excellent site for kids to visit and read information on eating disorders, healthy eating, exercise, and body image.

EXPERT PARENTS http://www.expertparents.com/index.html. This site provides good information about a multitude of topics, including eating disorders.

GRAMMA'S HOUSE http://grammashouse.net/. A welcome site that provides information about eating disorders after the user enters Gramma's House.

NATIONAL EATING DISORDERS ASSOCIATION http://www.nationaleating disorders.org. This association is the largest nonprofit eating disorders association in the United States. They distribute educational materials and have a toll-free information and referral line at 1-800-931-2237. They also have watchdog programs to help individuals get involved in changing the media's portrayal of dieting, food, and the drive for thinness.

THE RENFREW CENTER FOUNDATION www.renfrew.org and the RENFREW CENTER www.renfrewcenter.com. The foundation site provides download-able information about eating disorders, suggests way to help combat eat-ing disorders, and helps the user locate her U.S. Representatives so she can voice her concerns about the prevalence of eating disorders. The center's site provides information about treatment options and their facilities.

SOMETHING FISHY WEBSITE ON EATING DISORDERS http://www.something-fishy.org/. The creators of this site disseminate information about recovery, reach out to others with eating disorders, and raise awareness that recovery is possible. They stress that eating disorders are not about food and weight but about emotional issues. This site also helps link the client to counselors or psychologists who specialize in eating-disorder treatment.

REFERENCES

———————————— • ————————————

Abrams, K., Allen, L., & Gray, J. (1993). Disordered eating attitudes and be-
    haviors, psychological adjustment, and ethnic identity: A comparison
    of Black and White female college students. *International Journal of
    Eating Disorders, 14,* 49–57.
American Psychiatric Association. (2000). *Diagnostic and statistical manual
    of mental disorders* (4th ed., Rev. ed.). Washington, DC: American
    Psychiatric Association.
Anderson, A. E., & DiDomenico, L. (1992). Diet vs. shape content of popu-
    lar male and female magazines: A dose-response relationship to the in-
    cidence of eating disorders? *International Journal of Eating Disorders,
    11*(3), 283–287.
Austin, E. W., & Johnson, K. K. (1997). Effects of general and alcohol-specific
    media literacy training on children's decision making about alcohol.
    Journal of Health Communication, 2(1), 17–43.
Austin, E. W., & Meili, H. K. (1994). Effects of interpretation of televised al-
    cohol portrayals on children's alcohol beliefs. *Journal of Broadcasting
    and Electronic Media,* 418–435.
Babbitt, R. L., Edlen-Nezin, L., Manikam, R., Summers, J. A., & Murphy,
    C. M. (1995). Assessment of eating and weight-related problems in
    children and special populations. In D. B. Allison (Ed.), *Handbook
    of assessment methods for eating behaviors and weight-related prob-
    lems: Measures, theory, and research* (pp. 431–492). London: Sage
    Publications.
Berel, S., & Irving, L. M. (1998). Media and disturbed eating: An analysis of
    media influence and implications for prevention. *The Journal of Primary
    Prevention, 18*(4), 415–430.

Bloom, C., Gitter, A., Gutwill, S., Kogel, L., & Zaphiropoulos, L. (1999). The truth about dieting: A feminist view. In R. Lemberg & L. Cohn (Eds.), *Eating disorders: A reference sourcebook* (pp. 61–64). Phoenix: Oryx Press.

Body Image Advertising (2000). Retrieved February 22, 2004, from http://www.mediascope.org/pubs/ibriefs/bia.htm.

Bourne, E. D. (1995). *The anxiety and phobia workbook.* Oakland, CA: New Harbinger.

Bruch, H. (1978). *The golden cage: The enigma of anorexia nervosa.* Cambridge: Harvard University Press.

Bushnell, J. A., Wells, J. E., & Oakley-Brown, M. A. (1992). Long-term effects of intrafamilial sexual abuse in childhood. *Acta Psychiatrica Scandinavica, 85,* 136–142.

Calam, R. M., & Slade, P. D. (1989). Sexual experience and eating problems in female undergraduates. *International Journal of Eating Disorders, 8,* 391–397.

Carter, J., Stewart, D., Dunn, V., & Fairburn, C. (1997). Primary prevention of eating disorders: Might it do more harm than good? *International Journal of Eating Disorders, 22,* 167–173.

Cash, T. F., & Strachan, M. D. (1999). Body images, eating disorders, and beyond. In R. Lemberg & L. Cohn (Eds.), *Eating disorders: A reference sourcebook* (pp. 27–37). Phoenix: Oryx Press.

Cavanaugh, C. J., & Lemberg, R. (1999). What we know about eating disorders: Facts and statistics. In R. Lemberg & L. Cohn (Eds.), *Eating disorders: A reference sourcebook* (pp. 7–12). Phoenix: Oryx Press.

Costin, C. (1999). *The eating disorder sourcebook: A comprehensive guide to the causes, treatments, and prevention of eating disorders* (2nd ed.). Los Angeles: Lowell House.

Creager, E. (2002, November 27). To buy or not to buy? Barbie bares her belly; can parents bear it? *Detroit Free Press.* Retrieved November 15, 2003, from http://www.freep.com/money/business/barbie27_20021127.htm

Dalle Grave, R. (2003). School-based prevention programs for eating disorders: Achievements and opportunities. *Dis Manage Health Outcomes, 11*(9), 579–593.

Dansky, B. S., Brewerton, T. D., Kilpatrick, D. G., & O'Neil, P. M. (1997). Rape PTSD and bulimia in a U.S. sample of women. *International Journal of Eating Disorders, 21,* 213–228.

Dare, C., & Crowther, C. (1995). Psychodynamic models of eating disorders. In G. Szmukler, C. Dare, & J. Treasure (Eds.), *Handbook of eat-*

ing disorders: Theory, treatment and research (pp. 125–139). New York: John Wiley & Sons.

Davis, C., & Katzman, M. A. (1999). Perfection as acculturation: Psychological correlates of eating problems in Chinese male and female students living in the United States. *International Journal of Eating Disorders, 25*(1), 65–70.

Demarest, J., & Allen, R. (2000). Body image: Gender, ethnic, and age differences. *Journal of Social Psychology, 140*(4). Retrieved October 5, 2003, from EBSCOhost website: http://web12.epnet.com/citation.asp

De Silva, P. (1995). Cognitive-behavioural models of eating disorders. In G. Szmukler, C. Dare, & J. Treasure (Eds.), *Handbook of eating disorders: Theory, treatment and research* (pp. 141–153). New York: John Wiley & Sons.

Dittrich, L. (1996). *About-Face facts on the media. About-Face facts on body image. About-Face facts on eating disorders.* Retrieved October 1, 2003, from http://www.about-face.org/resources/facts/media.html

Dolan, B. (1994). Why women? Gender issues and eating disorders: Introduction. In B. Dolan & I. Gitzinger (Eds.), *Why women? Gender issues and eating disorders* (pp. 1–11). London: Athlone Press.

Dolan, B., & Gitzinger, I. (1994). *Why women? Gender issues and eating disorders.* London: Athlone Press.

Eisler, I. (1995). Family models of eating disorders. In G. Szmukler, C. Dare, & J. Treasure (Eds.), *Handbook of eating disorders: Theory, treatment and research* (pp. 155–176). New York: John Wiley & Sons.

Fairburn, C. (1995). *Overcoming binge eating.* New York: Guilford Press.

Fairburn, C. (1997). Eating disorders. In D. Clark & C. Fairburn (Eds.), *Science and practice of cognitive behaviour therapy* (pp. 209–241). Oxford: Oxford University Press.

Faludi, S. (1991). *Backlash: The undeclared war against American women.* New York: Crown Publishers, Inc.

Fedoroff, I. C., & McFarlane, T. (1998). Cultural aspects of eating disorders. In S. S. Kazarian & D. R. Evans (Eds.), *Cultural clinical psychology: Theory, research, and practice* (pp. 152–176). New York: Oxford University Press.

Folkman, S., & Lazarus, R. S. (1985). If it changes it must be a process: Study of emotion and coping during three stages of a college examination. *Journal of Personality and Social Psychology, 48,* 150–170.

Friedman, S. S. (1998). Girls in the 90s: A gender-based model for eating disorder prevention. *Patient Education and Counseling, 33,* 217–224.

Garfinkel, P. E., & Lin, E. (1995). Bulimia nervosa in a Canadian community sample: Prevalence and comparison of subgroups. *American Journal of Psychiatry, 152*(7), 1052–1059.

Ghaderi, A. (2001). Review of risk factors for eating disorders: Implication for primary prevention and cognitive behavioural therapy. *Scandinavian Journal of Behaviour Therapy, 30*(2), 57–74.

Gladding, S. T. (1999). *Group work: A counseling speciality* (3rd ed.). Upper Saddle River, New Jersey: Merrill.

Gowen, L. K., & Hayward, C. (1999). Acculturation and eating disorder symptoms in adolescent girls. *Journal of Research on Adolescence, 9*(1). Retrieved October 5, 2003, from EBSCOhost website: http://web12.epnet.com/citation.asp

Halstead, M., Johnson, S. B., & Cunningham, W. (1993). Measuring coping in adolescents: An application of the ways of coping checklist. *Journal of Clinical Child Psychology, 22*(3), 337–344.

Hastings, T., & Kern, J. M. (1994). Relationships between bulimia, child-hood sexual abuse and family environment. *International Journal of Eating Disorders, 15*(2), 103–111.

Irving, L. M. (1990). Mirror images: Effects of the standard of beauty on the self- and body-esteem of women exhibiting various levels of bulimic symptoms. *Journal of Social and Clinical Psychology, 9*(2), 230–242.

Jackson, C. (2003). *Meet Cindy Jackson*. Retrieved April 22, 2003, from http://www.cindyjackson.com.

Jacob, A. (2001). Body image distortion and eating disorders: No longer a 'culture-bound' topic . *Healthy Weight Journal, 15*(6). Retrieved October 5, 2003, from EBSCOhost website: http://web12.epnet.com/citation.asp

Johnson, C. (1995). Psychodynamic treatment of bulimia nervosa. In K. D. Brownell & C. G. Fairburn (Eds.), *Eating disorders and obesity: A comprehensive handbook* (pp. 349–353). New York: Guilford Press.

Jones, K. (1997). History and prevention of eating disorders. *The Prevention Researcher, 4*(3), 1–11.

Kilbourne, J. (1995). *Slim hopes videorecording: Advertising and the obsession with thinness* [motion picture]. (Available from Northampton, MA).

Kinoy, B. P., Holman, A. M., & Lemberg, R. (1999). The eating disorders: An introduction. In R. Lemberg & L. Cohn (Eds.), *Eating disorders: A reference sourcebook* (pp. 2–6). Phoenix: Oryx Press.

Levine, M. P. (1999). Prevention of eating disorders, eating problems, and negative body image. In R. Lemberg & L. Cohn (Eds.), *Eating disorders: A reference sourcebook* (pp. 64–72). Phoenix: Oryx Press.

Levine, M. P., Smolak, L., & Hayden, H. (1994). The relation of sociocultural factors to eating attitudes and behaviors among middle school girls. *Journal of Early Adolescence, 14*, 471–490.

Maloney, M. J. (1988). Reliability testing of the Children's Version of the Eating Attitudes Test. *Journal of the American Academy of Child and Adolescent Psychiatry, 27*, 542–543.

Martin, M. C., & Kennedy, P F. (1993). Advertising and social comparison: Consequences for female preadolescents and adolescents. *Psychology and Marketing, 10*, 513–530.

Miars, R. D. (1996). Stress and coping in today's society. In D. Capuzzi & D. R. Gross (Eds.), *Youth at risk: A prevention resource for counselors, teachers, and parents* (pp. 129–145). Alexandria, VA: American Counseling Association.

Miller, D. A. F., McCluskey-Fawcett, K., & Irving, L. M. (1993). The relationship between childhood sexual abuse and subsequent onset of bulimia nervosa. *Child Abuse and Neglect: The International Journal, 17*, 305–314.

Mussell, M. P., Mitchell, J. E., Fenna, C. J., Crosby, R. D., Miller, J. P., & Hoberman, H. M. (1997). A comparison of onset of binge eating versus dieting in the development of bulimia nervosa. *The International Journal of Eating Disorders, 21*(4), 353–360.

National Broadcasting Company. (n.d.). The more you know. *NBC Public Service Announcement Series*. Available at http://www.nbc.com/nbc/footer/tmyk/pgv_moreabout_didyouknow.shtml.

Neumark-Sztainer, D. (1996). School based program for the prevention of eating disturbances. *The Journal of School Health, 66*, 64–71.

O'Dea, J. (2001). Activities to improve the body image and prevent eating problems in children—A self-esteem approach. *Primary Educator, 7*(2). Retrieved October 5, 2003, from EBSCOhost website: http://web12.epnet.com/citation.asp.

O'Dea, J. (2002). The new self-esteem approach for the prevention of body image and eating problems in children and adolescents. *Healthy Weight Journal, 16*(6). Retrieved October 5, 2003, from EBSCOhost website: http://web12.epnet.com/citation.asp.

Pacific Science Center. (2001). *Nutrition Café*. Retrieved May 28, 2003, from http://www.exhibitspacsci.org/nutrition.

Pageant News Bureau. (1995). Alicia Machado, Armi Kuusela, Linda Bennent. Retrieved April 22, 2003, from http://www.pageant.com.

Pate, J. E., Pumariega, A. J., Hester, C., & Garner, D. M. (1992). Cross-cultural patterns in eating disorders: A review. *Journal of the American Academy of Child and Adolescent Psychiatry, 31*(5), 802–809.

Perry, C. L., Story, M., & Lytle, L. A. (1997). Promoting healthy dietary be-
haviors (Report No. PS 026 199). *In Enhancing Children's Wellness.
Healthy Children 2010.* Retrieved from ERIC Document Reproduction
Service (ED 416966).

Petersons, M., Rojhani, A., Steinhaus, N., & Larkin, B. (2000). Effect of ethnic identity on attitudes, feelings, and behaviors toward foods. *Eating
Disorders, 8,* 207–219.

Pipher, M. (1994). *Reviving Ophelia: Saving the selves of adolescent girls.* New
York: Ballantine Books.

Ressler, A. (1999, March). *Eating disorders: The pursuit of perfection.* Profes-
sional Development Workshop Presented by the Florida Counseling
Association. St. Thomas University, Florida.

Rhyne-Winkler, M. C., & Hubbard, G. T. (1994). Eating attitudes and behavior: A school counseling program. *The School Counselor, 41,*
195–198.

Richins, M. L. (1991). Social comparison and the idealized images of advertising. *Journal of Consumer Research, 18,* 71–83.

Robinson, P. H., & McHugh, P. R. (1995). A physiology of starvation that
sustains eating disorders. In G. Szmukler, C. Dare, & J. Treasure
(Eds.), *Handbook of eating disorders: Theory, treatment and research*
(pp. 109–123). New York: John Wiley & Sons.

Sands, R., Tricker, J., Sherman, C., Armatas, C., & Maschette, W. (1997).
Disordered eating patterns, body image, self-esteem, and physical ac-
tivity in preadolescent school children. *International Journal of Eating
Disorders, 21*(2), 159–166.

Sharpe, T. M., Ryst, E., Hinshaw, S. P., & Steiner, H. (1997). Reports of
stress: A comparison between eating disordered and non-eating disordered adolescents. *Child Psychiatry and Human Development, 28*(2),
117–132.

Silverstein, B., Perdue, L., Peterson, B., & Kelly, E. (1986). The role of the
mass media in promoting a thin standard of bodily attractiveness for
women. *Sex Roles, 14*(9/10), 519–532.

Srebnik, D. S., & Saltzberg, E. A. (1994). Feminist cognitive-behavioral therapy for negative body-image. *Women and Therapy, 15*(2), 117–133.

Steiger, H., & Zanko, M. (1990). Sexual traumata among eating disordered,
psychiatric, and normal female groups. *Journal of Interpersonal Violence,
5,* 74–86.

Steiner, H., & Lock, J. (1998). Anorexia nervosa and bulimia nervosa in
children and adolescents: A review of the past 10 years. *Journal of
the American Academy of Child and Adolescent Psychiatry, 37*(4),
352–359.

Stice, E., & Shaw, H. E. (1994). Adverse effects of the media portrayed thin-ideal on women and linkages to bulimic symptomatology. *Journal of Social and Clinical Psychology, 13,* 288–308.

Streigel-Moore, R. H. (1995). A feminst perspective on the etiology of eating disorders. In K. D. Brownell & C. G. Fairburn (Eds.), *Eating disorders and obesity: A comprehensive handbook* (pp. 224–229). New York: Guilford Press.

Strober, M. (1995). Family-genetic perspectives on anorexia nervosa and bulimia nervosa. In K. D. Brownell & C. G. Fairburn (Eds.), *Eating disorders and obesity: A comprehensive handbook* (pp. 212–218). New York: Guilford Press.

Treasure, J., & Holland, A. (1995). Genetic factors in eating disorders. In G. Szmukler, C. Dare, & J. Treasure (Eds.), *Handbook of eating disorders: Theory, treatment and research* (pp. 65–81). New York: John Wiley & Sons.

Vandereycken, W. (1995). The families of patients with an eating disorder. In K. D. Brownell & C. G. Fairburn (Eds.), *Eating disorders and obesity: A comprehensive handbook* (pp. 219–223). New York: Guilford Press.

Wonderlich, S. A., Brewerton, T. D., Jocic, Z., Dansky, B. S., & Abbott, D. W. (1997). Relationship of childhood sexual abuse and eating disorders. *Journal of the American Academy of Child and Adolescent Psychiatry, 36*(8), 1107–1115.

Wonderlich, S., & Donaldson, M. A. (1996). Eating disturbance and incest. *Journal of Interpersonal Violence, 11*(2), 195–207.

Wright, K. S. (1996). The secret and all-consuming obsessions: Anorexia and bulimia. In D. Capuzzi & D. R. Gross (Eds.), *Youth at risk: A prevention resource for counselors, teachers, and parents* (pp. 153–178). Alexandria, VA: American Counseling Association.

Zabinsky, M. F., Pung, M. A., Wilfley, D. E., Eppstein, D. L., Winzelberg, A. J., Celio, A. et al. (2001). Reducing risk factors for eating disorders: Targeting at-risk women with a computerized psychoeducational program. *International Journal of Eating Disorders, 29*(4), 401–409.

Index

About-Face, 41, 43, 73–74, 78
acculturation, levels of, 27–28
advertisements, 10, 12, 15, 22, 30, 31, 41–45, 73–74
Angelou, Maya, 1, 25
anorexia nervosa
    abstract reasoning and, 6
    common characteristics, 2–3
    depression and, 7
    diagnostic criteria, 2, 90
    etiology (*see* etiology of eating disorders)
    faulty cognitions, 8
    history, 1–3
    as a learned behavior, 8
    norephinephrine, 7
    obsessive-compulsive disorder and, 7
    positive reinforcement and, 8
    puberty and, 6
    relational self and, 6
    seratonin, 7
    sexual abuse and, 5–6
    sociocultural factors, 7
    statistics, 20

stress and, 7, 11, 22–23, 47–50
    why now, 9
art therapy, 20
Association for Specialists in Group Work, 29

Barbie, 18, 73
beauty pageants, 15
Bement, Linda, 52
biochemical theory, 7–8
Body Armor prevention program
    cofacilitators and, 34–35
    confidentiality agreement, 63
    confidentiality and, 34
    empowerment and, 57
    goals and objectives, 62
    group leader, evaluation of, 67–68
    group leader's role, 29
    Internet, 15
    inventories and, 34–35, 59
    invitation for parents, 69
    parental involvement and, 32–34, 59
    parent/guardian permission form, 62

Body Armor prevention program
  (*continued*)
  parent/guardian questionnaire,
    64
  pledge sheet, 83
  risks involved in, 36
  session overviews, 30–32
  skits, presentations, 57–59
  stress relief and, 23, 31, 47–49,
    82
  structure of, 29–30
  target audience, 26–27
body image
  acceptance of, 51
  activity, 51–53
  art therapy and, 20
  beauty, 9, 10, 12, 18, 19, 53
  cognitive distortions and, 8
  cognitive restructuring and, 14
  cosmetic surgery and, 19, 52
  definition of beauty and, 9–10
  developmental issues and, 52
  dieting and, 21
  ethnicity and, 27–28
  fashion models and, 41, 72
  masculine versus feminine, 4
  media images and, 18–19, 39, 51,
    73–74
  puberty and, 6, 7
  self-esteem and, 10–11, 19–20
  social messages and, 20–21
  social status and, 19
  visual representation of, 51
Body Shop, 72, 74
body type, 4, 14, 15, 27, 54
breaking-the-code activity, 41, 75
breathing technique, 50, 84
bulimia nervosa, 3, 4, 5, 7, 8, 21, 26
  diagnostic criteria, 3, 90

Chic jeans ad, 74
Children's Version of the Eating At-
    titudes Test, 40, 59, 65–66
Christian Dior, 74
cofacilitators, 1, 29, 30–35, 37, 40,
    43, 47, 49, 52, 53, 56–59
cognitive behavioral model, 8
cognitive distortions, 8
confidentiality, 34, 40
confidentiality agreement, 63
cosmetic surgery, 19, 52, 88
cumulative stressor model, 23

developmental theory, 6–7
dieting
  body image perceptions, 21
  conflicting media messages and,
    45
  cycle of, 6, 21, 46
  dangers of, 22, 46
  diseases related to, 22
  futility of, 22
  good versus bad food, 22, 35,
    46
  industry, 21
  magazine advertising and, 22, 45,
    73
  media and, 12, 18
  natural solution, 22
  nutrition and, 20–22, 46
  risk factor for bulimia nervosa, 21
  statistics, 21
Disease-Specific Pathways model, 13
Disorder-Specific Continuity model,
    11, 15, 44, 50
dissonance-based approach, 13–14

eating disorders
  acculturation and, 27–28

African American women and, 27
age of onset, 26
anorexia (*see* anorexia nervosa)
Asian American women and, 28
bulimia (*see* bulimia nervosa)
culture-bound syndrome, 27
Hispanic women and, 27–28
mortality rates, 25
prevention (*see* prevention)
recovery, 25
resources, 98–99
risk factors (*see* risk factors)
stereotypical view, 27
viewed as a continuum, 11
women's increased power and, 9,
    19–20
ethical issues, 36
etiology of eating disorders
    biochemical theory, 7
    cognitive behavioral model, 8
    developmental theory, 6
    family model, 5–6
    feminist model, 9–11
    genetic model, 4–5
    psychodynamic model, 3–4
evaluation of group, 35

family model, 5–6
feminist model, 9–10, 11–12, 14,
    15, 19, 39, 42, 50, 55
fishbowl activity, 52–53
flapper, 20
food pyramid, 46, 80

gender roles, 19, 20
genetic model, 4–5
Girls in the '90s, 52
group leader, 1, 29
group members, 33

Gucci, 73
Gull, Sir William, 2

hormone
    cholecystokinin, 7
    vasopressin, 7

Internet, 14, 32, 49
invitation, 69

Jackson, Cindy, 52, 88

Kuusela, Armi, 52

Laseque, Charles, 2

Machado, Alicia, 45
magazines, fashion, 6, 9, 10–11, 15,
    17, 22, 41, 54, 74
marriage, 9, 22
media messages
    advertisements, 10, 22, 30, 31,
        41–45, 73–74
    challenging of, 15, 19
    children's clothing and, 26
    contradictory, 45
    decoding, 41, 43, 73–74
    disputing and voicing concerns
        about, 42–44
    image cropping, 73
    literacy, 17, 18
    starvation imagery, 14, 15, 19,
        54
    submissiveness and, 74
    television shows and, 9
meditation exercise, 50, 84–86
Miss Universe, 45, 52
Moschino, 73
Monroe, Marilyn, 20

National Eating Disorders Association, 43, 78, 96, 99

NBC's *The More You Know*, 31, 55–57, 58, 94

"New Self-Esteem Approach," 54

Nonspecific Life Stress model, 11, 15, 47

Nonspecific Vulnerability Stressor model, 13

norephinephrine, 7

normative stressor model, 23

nutrition, 12, 15, 16, 20, 21, 25, 46, 54, 56

Nutrition Café, 46

nutrition explorations, 46

nutrition model, 12

Panasonic, 74

parental involvement, 32–34, 58–59

parents and guardians, 3, 6, 7, 8, 11, 15, 16, 22, 31–34, 36, 37, 42, 53, 59

Participatory-Empowerment-Ecological Relational model, 14, 15, 42, 47, 53, 57, 58

PEER model (*see* Participatory-Empowerment-Ecological Relational model)

permission form, 62

preadolescent, 12, 22, 23, 25, 26, 29, 30

prevention theory and models
Body Armor Program, 15–16, 25–37
Disease-Specific Pathways model, 13
Disorder-Specific Continuity model, 11, 15, 44, 50

dissonance-based approach, 14

feminist model, 9–10, 11–12, 14, 15, 19, 39, 42, 50, 55

low-risk and high-risk participants, 36

Nonspecific Life Stress model, 11, 15, 47

Nonspecific Vulnerability Stressor model, 13

nutrition model, 12

Participatory-Empowerment-Ecological Relational model, 14, 15, 42, 47, 53, 57, 58

target programs, 13, 14

universal programs, 13, 14

psychodynamic theory, 3–4

psychoeducational group, 14, 29

puberty, 4, 6, 7, 23, 26, 51

questionnaires
Children's Version of the Eating Attitudes Test, 40, 59, 65–66
Cofacilitator Evaluation of the Group Leader, 67
for parent or guardian, 64

Real Women Have Curves, 28

Renfrew Center Foundation, 20, 41, 51, 96, 99

risk factors
body image, 19–20
determining risk factors, 12–13
dieting and nutrition, 20–22
media literacy, 17–19
self-esteem, 19–20
sociocultural factors, 9, 13
stress, 22–23

Ruby, 52, 72, 74

Schwartz, Morrie, 17
self-esteem, 9, 10, 11, 13, 14, 15,
    17, 19, 74
self-starvation
    religious atonement, 2
seratonin, 7
session overviews, 30–32
sexual abuse, 5–6
social learning skills, 15
sociocultural perspective, 9, 13
sociohistorical perspective, 19
starvation imagery, 14, 15, 19, 54
Steinem, Gloria, 39
stress
    causes and effects of, 48–49
    coping with, 15–16, 22–23, 48,
        49, 82
    decision making and, 52
    emotions and, 49
    meditation and, 50, 84–86
    pledge sheet, 83
structure of the group, 29–30

talking stick activity, 52–53
target audience, 26–28
target programs, 14
toys
    Barbie, 18, 73
    Diva Starz Mikki, 18

traumatic life events model, 23
Twiggy, 20

universal programs, 14

vasopressin, 7
Vogue magazine, 41

watchdogs, 16, 42, 44, 46, 78
websites
    About-Face, 41, 73, 74, 78
    Chatelaine, 53
    Cindyjackson.com, 88
    Club Girl Tech, 49, 82, 96
    4 empowering websites,
        96–97
    4 Girls Health, 48, 55, 82
    Girl Zone, 49, 82, 97
    girls inc., 48, 55, 82, 91, 97
    Just 4 Girls, 48, 82
    kidfood.org, 80
    KidsHealth, 49, 82, 97
    National Eating Disorders, Asso-
        ciation 43, 78, 96, 99
    Something Fishy, 44, 99
weight loss, 2, 3, 8, 9, 21, 22
Woman's World magazine, 45

ABOUT THE AUTHOR

BEVERLY MENASSA holds a degree in mental health counseling and is a LPCI at North Central Texas College.